WE CAN RESCUE
OUR CHILDREN

WE CAN RESCUE OUR CHILDREN

The Cure for Chicago's Public School Crisis - With Lessons for the Rest of America

By

Herbert J. Walberg
Research Professor of Education
University of Illinois at Chicago

Michael J. Bakalis
Dean of the School of Education
Loyola University of Chicago

Joseph L. Bast
Executive Director
The Heartland Institute

Steven Baer
Executive Director
United Republican Fund of Illinois
and URF Education Foundation

A nonpartisan publication sponsored by:

URF Education Foundation
The Heartland Institute
Illinois Council on Democratic Policy

First published in 1988 by URF Education Founda-
tion, 320 North Michigan Avenue, Suite 23N,
Chicago, Illinois 60601, in cooperation with Green
Hill Publishers, Box 738, Ottawa, Illinois 61350.

Printed and bound in the United States of America.

91   90   89   88   5   4   3   2   1

ISBN 0-89803-160-5

To the children of Chicago.

CONTENTS

Part 3: The Cure

PREFACE

Serious social problems call forth cooperation that otherwise would be unlikely. Once convinced of the gravity of a problem, people who otherwise would be divided along political or ideological lines can come together to study the issues, understand the causes of the problem, and propose solutions they can all support.

Such was the case with this book. Two of the authors are academics, a third is with a partisan advocacy organization, and the fourth represents a nonpartisan research organization. One author is a prominent Democrat, another a well-known Republican. Out of these very different backgrounds and associations has come consensus on the nature of the problem and the correct direction for reform.

Authors

Michael J. Bakalis, dean of the School of Education at Loyola University, is the state chairman of the 1988 Illinois Dukakis for President Committee and former Illinois State Superintendent of Education. He is cofounder of the Illinois Council on Democratic Policy, a think tank for the Democratic Party of Illinois, and cochair of Chicagoans United to Reform Education (C.U.R.E.), a grassroots coalition for education reform in Chicago. His efforts on behalf of public education in Illinois have earned him many honors and awards, including the Presidential Citation of the Illinois Association of School Administrators, the PUSH Award for Excellence in Education, and the Illinois Association of School Boards Award for Distinguished Leadership.

Herbert J. Walberg, research professor of education at the University of Illinois at Chicago, is a distinguished educational researcher. The author or editor of thirty books and hundreds of articles in scholarly journals, Dr. Walberg is the nation's leading expert in the analysis of factors affecting educational productivity. He served as an advisor to Chicago's late Mayor Harold Washington and as a consultant or committee member for many Chicago and national civic groups. He has been an advisor to U.S. Secretary of Education William Bennett; to federal government agencies including the General Accounting Office, Congressional Budget Office, Department of State, and National Science Foundation; and to education officials in nine countries. Dr. Walberg has testified before U.S. Congressional committees and federal courts.

Joseph L. Bast has served as executive director of The Heartland Institute, a Chicago-based nonprofit and nonpartisan research organization, since its founding in April 1984. He has assembled a panel of over forty noted academics and business economists who submit research and participate in peer review procedures for The Heartland Institute. He is the editor or author of eighteen studies of state and local public policy, and his writings have appeared hundreds of times in newspapers throughout the Midwest.

Steven Baer is executive director of the United Republican Fund of Illinois and URF Education Foundation. His essays and articles have appeared in the *Columbia Journalism Review*, *National Review*, *Chicago Tribune*, *Chicago Sun-Times*, *The Washington Times*, and *Christianity Today*. A graduate of

Acknowledgements

This book is a product of the Education Policy Initiative, a discussion group involving leading thinkers and organizations in Illinois' education community. The group was convened in February 1987 by the URF Education Foundation, the nonpartisan educational affiliate of the United Republican Fund of Illinois. The authors benefited from the valuable advice and assistance of participants in the group; we would like to convey our deep appreciation and thanks to all of them.

The authors also benefited from access to the many resources of The Heartland Institute, United Republican Fund and URF Education Foundation, and Illinois Council on Democratic Policy. We wish to thank the staffs and supporters of these organizations for making this effort possible.

We are particularly indebted to John H. Beck, visiting associate professor of economics, Cleveland State University; Franklin M. Buchta, president, Heartland Wisconsin; George Clowes, president, Decision Support Enterprises; Louise Kaegi, writer and editorial consultant; John J. Lane, professor of education, DePaul University; David L. Littmann, first vice president and senior economist, Manufacturers National Bank (Detroit); Anne McCracken, secretary, American Federation of Small Business of Illinois; Everett Moffat, independent trader, Chicago Board Options Exchange; David H. Padden, president, The Heartland Institute; Daniel Polsby, professor of law, Northwestern University School of Law; and Roger Weiss, professor of social science, The University of Chicago. Each of these individuals read the entire manuscript and submitted many thoughtful suggestions. Diane Carol Bast, publications director for The Heartland Institute, edited every line of each early version of the manuscript, an enormous task and one that she performed with outstanding skill and dedication to clarity. Needless to say, these good friends are not responsible for whatever errors remain.

Many other people, some of them active participants in the Education Policy Initiative, provided valuable assistance during the research, writing, and editing of this publication. Not all of these people support every idea presented in this book, and some have expressed concerns about aspects of our proposed cure for Chicago's public school crisis. But we certainly benefited from their input, and would like to recognize them here:

Betty Bonow, former member of the Chicago Board of Education; John Buck, president, The John Buck Company; Jameson Campaigne, Jr., president, Green Hill Publishers; Allan Carlson, president, The Rockford Institute; Barry J. Carroll, vice president, Katy Industries, Inc. and former special assistant to the U.S. Secretary of Education, Terrel Bell; Robert Allan Cooke, director, Institute for Business Ethics; Joan M. Ferdinand, executive director, City Club of Chicago; Dren Geer, director, Academy of Educators; Robert J. Genetski, senior vice president and chief economist, Harris Trust and Savings Bank; Rev. Eddie Hathcoat, president, Christian Schools of Illinois; Denis J. Healy, president, Turtle Wax, Inc. and chairman of Options for People, Inc.; Sondra A. Healy, chairman, Turtle Wax, Inc.; James L. Johnston, senior economist, Amoco Corporation; Gary Laszewski, research associate, The Civic Federation; Daniel T. McCaffery, senior vice-president, BCE Development Properties, Inc.; Michael E. McCarthy, director, The New Asia Bank, and director, Consolidated Shares; Patrick T. Peterson, development director, The Heartland Institute; Illinois State

Representative Penny Pullen; Henry Regnery, chairman, Regnery Gateway, Inc.; Jack Roeser, president, Otto Engineering; J. Patrick Rooney, chairman, Golden Rule Insurance Company; Hans A. Schieser, professor of education, DePaul University; John W. Skorburg, director, government policy planning and analysis, Sears, Roebuck & Co.; Michael Smith, codirector, Save Our Neighborhoods/Save Our City Coalition; Richard Stein, chairman and chief executive, Stein & Company; Ann Stull, former Chicago Public Schools teacher; Dr. Roland Wesley, director, Carlinshar & Associates; Kent R.N. Whitney, former interval auditor and manager of accounting systems, City Colleges of Chicago Community College District 508; Kenneth T. Wright, president, United Republican Fund of Illinois and Easter Seal Society of Metropolitan Chicago, Inc.; John A. Zenko, president, Telemedia, Inc.

Publication of this book was originally planned for late Summer 1988. The Chicago teachers' strike of 1987 and resultant community efforts on behalf of school reform encouraged us to expedite the production schedule for this special preliminary paperback edition, thousands of which will be distributed in Chicago and throughout Illinois.

Although we are confident in our research and our conclusions, we recognize that any project of this scale, conducted on such an abbreviated schedule, can be improved and refined. We still intend to publish a definitive version of the book in several months. We invite all who have an opportunity to read this preliminary edition to submit their comments and concerns for possible incorporation into the future edition.

INTRODUCTION

Public education in Chicago is in a state of crisis. Our children are scoring far below national and international averages in reading and mathematics. Nearly half of the children who enroll in the schools drop out before graduating. Violence, teenage pregnancy, and drug abuse have become problems of alarming proportions.

The Chicago Public Schools have been given many opportunities for reform, but the system has failed. More money has not helped: Chicago spends nearly $4,000 per year per student on its public schools, more than the state and national averages and *three times* the amount spent at parochial schools. In 1986 the average teacher salary in Chicago was $31,000, some $5,000 higher than the average teacher salary downstate and again above the national average.

A few years ago the system had its staunch defenders. Now there is widespread agreement that fundamental structural reform is needed. Parents have deserted Chicago's public schools in record numbers since the 19-day teachers' strike in 1987. Organizations that campaigned regularly for more state funding of schools now say no more funds should be allocated until the system is overhauled. Federal, state, and local government officials have called for far-reaching reforms.

This book gives concerned citizens the facts about their public school system. It does not pull any punches, and it does not make excuses for the schools. Instead, the authors present a real cure: a two-step solution that would return authority to parents and communities, and would return to principals and teachers their self-respect as professionals.

Most importantly, step one of the cure would allow parents to choose the public school that best meets the needs of their children. We believe this measure is essential to restore accountability to our public schools. In making this recommendation we are challenging Chicago to join a nationwide movement toward voice and choice in public school systems.

As a further guarantee of good public schools in Chicago, three of the authors support step two of the solution: Education Rebates. Such a reform would give parents a "money back guarantee" that they will be able to enroll their child in a satisfactory school. The money back would take the form of a rebate for educational expenses paid in a nonpublic school or a public school of choice. This policy would empower Chicago's low-income parents and give the Chicago Public Schools further opportunity and incentive to excel.

Many of the problems afflicting the Chicago Public Schools plague the school systems of other large cities in America. Moreover, because of district consolidation and the gradual decline of parental involvement across the nation, many of these problems are beginning to affect smaller school systems in suburban and rural school districts. Chicago's problems and their cure should therefore be of great interest to parents and educators everywhere.

In Part One we show how public schools nationwide have been failing to produce satisfactory results, and how the Chicago Public Schools particularly have suffered from low test scores, high dropout rates, and lack of community involvement in curriculum. In Part Two we discover the sources of

2

these problems and consider the challenges posed by poverty and ethnic diversity in Chicago. We conclude that other school systems have faced these challenges and performed much better than have the Chicago Public Schools. In Part Three we describe a cure that addresses the historical causes of the problems. This blueprint for restructuring the schools promises to improve dramatically the quality of education in Chicago.

We believe education in Chicago can only be improved through structural reform. The purpose of this book is to provide a clear and compelling description of the kind of restructuring Chicago needs. But we seek much more than merely to bring the city's schools up to "the national average"; that would be the same as aspiring to mediocrity.

We envision nothing less than a renaissance in Chicago, propelled in large part by a dynamic and invigorated educational community: a Chicago that is known and respected around the world for the quality and diversity of its schools, the imagination and integrity of its leaders, and the skillfulness and knowledge of its graduating students.

There are those who say such a vision is utopian or unachievable. They say opposition from teachers unions will be too strong, or "political barriers" too great. To them we issue a simple challenge:

Read this book and talk to the teachers and parents who are already beginning Chicago's renaissance. Look again at the barriers that stand between us and the kind of school system our children need and deserve. Are these barriers so high that we should not try to scale them? Are they so great that we should stand to the side and complain, rather than join the concerned parents, teachers, and community leaders who have already started the necessary work? Is the road to reform not clearly marked?

To put it simply: we *can* rescue our children.

PART ONE

ARE THE CHICAGO PUBLIC SCHOOLS THE "WORST IN THE NATION"?

1

INSIDE THE CHICAGO PUBLIC SCHOOLS

> [M]ost of my neighbors are so disgusted with the Chicago Public School system that they will pay thousands of dollars a year in tuition rather than send their child to a public school.
>
> Cathy Greenwood
> Parent, Chicago's West Side

The Chicago businessmen who met with U.S. Secretary of Education William Bennett late in 1987 did not leave that session with a sense of ambiguity. The Secretary was direct, loud, and clear: Chicago's public schools, he said, are "the worst in the nation."

Whether in fact Chicago's public schools really are the worst, among the worst, or just very bad is unimportant. What is inescapably true is that many parents are dissatisfied with the city's public schools, and that a wide range of civic and community organizations have joined the call for "real reform."

In Chicago's schools there are men and women who by any definition are genuine heroes. They are the many dedicated and talented teachers who toil anonymously in the classrooms and there, against great odds, try to make a difference in children's lives. Yet the odds against succeeding are enormous.

In some settings a teacher's personal safety is at risk -- on any given day he might be the victim of a wildly swung fist or a knife, or even a bullet meant for someone else. Also at constant risk is a teacher's personal property: no purse can be left unguarded, no tape recorder left unattended. Ideally, no car should be parked where its owner cannot monitor it through a classroom window throughout the day.

But the students are not uniquely guilty in this conflict. Indeed, most are victims before they arrive at the schools. A large number are children of shattered homes or a culture drastically different from what they experience during much of the school day. Many are children of poverty, some of whom are shortchanged of the prerequisites for success before they begin the first day of school.

Students are faced with dozens of obstacles both outside and inside the school that threaten to draw them away from learning. Support for learning is often absent from their homes. The need for day-to-day economic survival makes schools seem a deterrent to getting money rather than an opportunity for the future. Peer pressures and gang activity push students in socially destructive directions or make them fear for their very lives. Drugs and pregnancy cut short youthful hopes and dreams.

With all these problems and more, Chicago's schools are filled with thousands of children who want to learn and thousands of competent men and women who genuinely want to teach them. But the number of teachers willing to come back each year is diminishing. Eventually the weariness, the burnout, the depression, the disappointment, the anger, and the pessimism wear them down. Trained as teachers, not warriors, much of their careers are spent battling anonymous, distant bureaucracies and the accumulation of all of society's problems.

Some teachers leave the profession and find other work. Too many stay in the classroom although they long ago left the profession. As one teacher recently put it, "There comes a time when you simply give up when you realize you're part of a losing team." And when we look at the scope and depth of the failure of the Chicago schools there can be little doubt that the system as a whole is indeed a losing team.

Standardized Test Scores

A wide disparity exists in academic achievement and reading scores between students in Chicago and the surrounding suburban school districts. In 1982, only 2.9 percent of Chicago high schools (two schools out of seventy) scored above the national average in reading, and in 1983 only 7 percent (five schools out of seventy) scored above the national average. In the suburbs, however, *every* reporting school scored at or above the national average.[1]

The Chicago picture becomes even more disheartening when we focus on students rather than schools. A report on the Chicago Class of 1984 indicates that only one out of three high school seniors could read at or above the national average. Only one freshman in four in the Class of 1987 could read at or above the national average.[2]

ACT and SAT scores are further indicators of student achievement -- and failure. Between 1969 and 1982, the *Illinois* scores on the ACT and SAT were slightly above the national norm, and since then they have remained stable.[3] In 1986 the typical Illinois student had an ACT composite score of 19.1 compared to a national average score of 18.8.[4]

The average *Chicago* high school student in 1986 had a dismal ACT composite score of just 13.6, some 28 percent below the national average. Only two high schools (Lane Tech and Young Magnet) out of sixty-four with students taking the tests managed average scores above the national and state averages, and both of these schools have selective admissions policies. In nine schools, not one student in the sophomore class scored in the top 25 percent nationally on any of the four exams that make up the ACT composite score.[5]

Dropout Rates

Between 43 and 53 percent of students who enter Chicago public high schools never graduate. In some schools the noncompletion rate is above 75 percent. In contrast, suburban Cook County noncompletion rates range from less than 10 percent to 36 percent, while statewide the average dropout rate is 24 percent. Thus, the dropout rate for the Chicago public schools is nearly double the state average.[6]

These numbers, of course, count only those students who have officially left school. On any given day in Chicago, more than thirty-five thousand students (8 percent of total enrollment) are missing from their classrooms, and about one-third of these are chronically truant.[7] Though not technically dropouts, there is little doubt these students have left their schools behind.

One reason students drop out of the public schools is fear of violence. They are right to be afraid. In 1986, 737 violent crimes were reported in Chicago public schools or on school grounds. This total included 559 serious assaults, 151 robberies, and twenty-seven criminal sexual assaults. In 1987 two students were murdered in their schools: Dartagnan Young, age fifteen, and Larry Sims, age sixteen.[8] The schools employ nearly five hundred security guards to patrol the halls and school grounds, and an additional 164 armed city police officers are assigned to the schools.[9]

One would expect that school dropouts, facing the hard realities of making it in the world, would see their decision to leave school as a mistake. Common sense suggests that they should reflect on their decision, regret dropping out, and realize that their ability to succeed is severely limited without the basic credential of a high school diploma. But in Chicago, there is little evidence of regret.

Thirty-five percent of respondents to a recent survey of dropouts in Illinois believed their decision to leave school had been a mistake, 28 percent were uncertain about the decision, and a full 37 percent reported that dropping out of school was a good decision. Thus, only about one-third of the dropouts expressed clear regrets about leaving school. Illinois' dropouts, it seems, do not even look back at the schools they leave.

Teachers' Choice

Perhaps the harshest indictment of Chicago public school education, however, is the number of public school teachers who choose to enroll their own children in private schools. The students teachers care about most -- their own children -- are not entrusted to the public school system.

Chicago public school teachers who live in the city are *twice* as likely as all other parents to send their children to private schools. Forty-six percent of the children of Chicago Public Schools teachers who live in the city attend private schools, as compared to only 22 percent of all school-age children in Chicago.[10]

Significantly, when Chicago Public Schools teachers live in suburban Cook County, they are much more likely to enroll their children in public schools. These teachers, who know the system best, who work in it and see it operate every day, are

11

apparently unwilling to risk *their* children's futures in such an ineffective system.

Bureaucracy

As part of their Chicago itinerary, two recent visitors from Japan were scheduled to tour the main offices of the Chicago Board of Education. When they arrived at the massive complex at 1819 West Pershing Road, they asked their American hosts a question: Was this, they inquired, the site of the U.S. Department of Education? To their amazement they discovered that this enormous, bureaucratic structure was merely the administrative offices of the schools of one city. In their own country, they said, the offices of the Japanese National Ministry of Education are not as large as the headquarters of the Chicago Public Schools.[11]

The Chicago Public Schools bureaucracy is indeed enormous. Approximately 3,300 employees assigned to the central and district offices create and perform an intricate array of administrative tasks.[12] None of them works in a school or teaches. This is in striking contrast to the *thirty-six* central office administrators employed by the Catholic Archdiocese, which serves a much larger geographic area.[13] Although the public schools serve two-and-one-half times as many students as do the Catholic schools, the former employ almost *one hundred* times as many administrators.

Between 1976 and 1986, student enrollment in the public school system fell by 18 percent. During that same period, the number of classroom teachers fell by 8 percent, but the number of teachers assigned to the central and district offices rose by 30 percent, from 2,107 to 2,736. None of these "teachers" actually teaches in a classroom. The number of school employees providing "support services" rose 47 percent during this period (from 564 to 828), and the number of administrators also rose 47 percent (from

12

383 to 563). These numbers do not include such career service employees as school clerks, engineers, janitors, or lunchroom workers.[14]

The Chicago Public Schools are an almost perfect case study of bureaucracy. Sociologist Max Weber, describing the outcomes of bureaucracies in his classic book on the subject, could just as well have been describing the Chicago Public Schools when he wrote:

> Language, once the means for bringing people into communication, becomes the secretive tool of one-way commands. Politics, especially democratic politics, fades away as the method of publicly determining society-wide goals based on human needs; it is replaced by administration.[15]

In fact, the Chicago school system has become a system in which no one seems to be accountable to anyone for anything; a system that has become unresponsive to people or to change and is conspicuously void of creativity; a system defensive against criticism; a system that seems to have lost faith in the clientele it is mandated to serve -- the students; and a system seemingly defiant of those who pay for its very existence -- the taxpayers of Chicago and Illinois.

This disregard for the students and the taxpayers is made possible by an environment in which both groups are given few choices. Too often their concerns are ignored, or they are given exercises in classic bureaucratic "run-around," sent from office to office and from person to person, who each in turn directs them to yet another person in yet another office. Thus, the very people who own and operate the schools through their taxes have, in practice, no control over them.

Spending Levels

Quality education costs money; no one doubts or disputes that. But this is quite different from saying that the solution to low-quality education is always to spend more money. Parents and taxpayers have heard the appeal for more money for Chicago's schools many times over the years, and they have responded generously.

Chicago does not shortchange its schools. General Fund revenues per pupil in 1987 were $3,915, which earned Chicago a rank of nineteenth among the nation's fifty largest school districts.[16] City spending per pupil in 1985-86 was over $600 more than the statewide average.[17] Statewide spending, in turn, is consistently above national averages. Among the fifty states and the District of Columbia, Illinois ranked twenty-second in public school expenditures per pupil and tenth in estimated average teacher salaries in 1986.[18] These are hardly the rankings of a state that has failed to invest adequately in its schools.

In 1985-86, the mean salary for a full-time Chicago public school teacher was $31,050, nearly $4,000 more than the statewide mean salary and over $5,000 more than the downstate mean salary.[19] This higher salary was paid despite the fact that Chicago teachers are less likely to hold advanced degrees and typically receive teaching degrees from the least selective teacher training colleges in the state. Almost half (40 percent) of Chicago teachers employed in 1983-84 came from these schools, compared with just 3 percent in the suburbs.[20]

A matter of concern for many years in Illinois has been the proportion of education funding that comes from the State. In Chicago, however, this should not be an issue. In 1983-84, the State provided 49 percent of Chicago Public Schools revenues, compared to just 32 percent each for Kane, Will, and the rest of Cook County, 15 percent for DuPage, 19 percent for Lake, and 24 percent for McHenry.[21] In

1987, over 50 percent of General Fund revenues for Chicago's public schools came from the State.[22]

If more money could solve Chicago's public school woes, the problems would have been solved by now. In fact, the source of the problems must lie elsewhere.

Conclusion

It hardly is surprising, in light of the facts presented in this chapter, that citizens who are polled report overall satisfaction with Illinois schools, but grade the Chicago Public Schools in the range of C- to D+.[23] In fact, only a meager 4 percent of Chicago residents believe their public schools are better than schools elsewhere in Illinois. Ninety-six people out of one hundred do not believe their schools are better than other schools in the state. Tragically, this represents an appropriate reaction to undeniable facts.

The success of a school system can be measured in many ways. Are the graduates humane, civilized, cultured individuals? Do they fulfill their responsibilities as citizens in a democracy? Have they acquired those skills, attitudes, and abilities that will allow them to be lifelong learners? All of these questions address essential aspects of the impact of education on people. However, few are systematically measured in any educational system. Instead, we must rely on those outputs that are concrete and measurable: standardized test scores, dropout rates, and spending levels. Chicago's public schools fail in each of these.

How could such a tragedy befall us? How can we literally walk across a street to leave Chicago, enter Evanston or Oak Park, and enter far superior schools? To answer these questions we must first know how public schools elsewhere are faring. Knowing whether the problems afflicting the Chicago Public Schools are unique to us or are shared by public schools across the nation will help guide us to effective reform.

1. Gary Orfield, *The Chicago Study of Access and Choice in Higher Education* (Chicago: University of Chicago Press), p. 136.
2. Designs for Change, *The Bottom Line: Chicago's Failing Schools and How to Save Them* (Chicago, 1985), pp. 11, 14.
3. Historically, the ACT is taken by more Illinois students than the SAT: in 1984, 106,586 high school seniors took the ACT, while in 1983 only 21,535 took the SAT. See *College Aptitude Test Scores* (Springfield, IL: Illinois State Board of Education, 1982), pp. 2-3.
4. John N. Maclean, "U.S. Gives Nation's Schools a 'C'," *Chicago Tribune*, February 11, 1987.
5. Casey Banas, "Schools' Report Card Shows City Lag," *Chicago Tribune*, October 16, 1986.
6. Designs for Change, p. 9.
7. *Chicago Tribune*, October 28, 1985.
8. Patrick Reardon and Casey Banas, "Schools Not So Perilous, Data Show," *Chicago Tribune*, December 11, 1987.
9. *Chicago Tribune*, May 5, 1985.
10. *Chicago Tribune*, May 3, 1984.
11. Harold Henderson, "The City File," *Reader* (Chicago), October 9, 1987.
12. Casey Banas, "Enrollment's Down, Office Workers Up," *Chicago Tribune*, September 29, 1987. Banas reported 2,736 teacher-certified employees working in the central and district offices, and another 563 administrators, directors, coordinators, and supervisors. The total is 3,299.
13. Archdiocese of Chicago, *Chicago Catholic Schools*, 1987-88 Report.
14. Casey Banas, "Enrollment's Down, Office Workers Up."
15. Ralph Hummel, *The Bureaucratic Experience* (New York: St. Martin's Press, 1977), p. 3.

16. "The Top 50 School Districts," *City and State*, October 1987.
17. Casey Banas, "Schools' Report Card Shows City Lag."
18. U.S. Dept. of Education, *State Education Statistic Supplement: Student Performance and Resource Inputs, 1986 and 1987*, Office of Planning, Budget, and Evaluation, February 1988.
19. Illinois State Board of Education, *Illinois Teacher Salary Schedule and Policy Study, 1985-86.*
20. *Chicago Tribune*, September 16, 1984.
21. Illinois State Board of Education, Department of Finance and Reimbursements.
22. "The Top 50 School Districts."
23. Herbert J. Walberg and G. Alfred Hess, Jr., *Chicagoans View Their Public Schools* (Chicago: Chicago Panel on Public School Finances, June 1985); Illinois Project for School Reform; and the Center for Governmental Studies, Northern Illinois University, "1984 Illinois Policy Survey."

2

A NATION AT RISK

The educational foundations of our society are presently being eroded by a rising tide of mediocrity that threatens our very future as a Nation and a people.

National Commission on Excellence in Education
A Nation at Risk

The Chicago Public Schools are unacceptable, but to some extent their problems are only a reflection of a nationwide decline in public education. A look at public schooling nationwide reveals a growing concern for low test scores, rising costs, and other problems well-known in Chicago.

Standardized Test Scores

Declining SAT scores have alerted the public to the possible declines in student performance.[1] Test scores in public schools throughout the U.S. fell substantially during the 1960s and 1970s; since 1980

Trends in SAT Scores
1962-63 to 1986-87

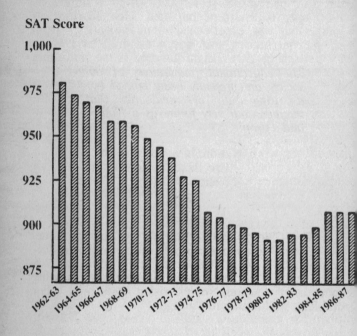

SAT Score

Source: U.S. Department of Education, February 1988.

there has been a stabilization in test scores and some modest increases. This record, particularly when compared to the performance of other nations or the performance of private schools in the U.S., paints a very sad picture of public schools.

Between 1963, when average combined SAT scores were at their highest, and 1980, the average verbal score fell 11 percent (fifty-four points) and the average mathematics score fell 7 percent (thirty-six points). In 1966, 2.5 percent of students taking the SAT had verbal scores over seven hundred; by 1981 only 0.8 percent obtained such scores. A similar fall was experienced in mathematics: from 4.1 percent scoring over seven hundred in 1966 to 2.7 percent in 1981. (Eight hundred is the maximum score for each of the two parts of the SAT tests.)[2]

Average test scores increased sixteen points from 1980 to 1985, but there has been little change since then. Responding to test scores announced in early 1988, U.S. Secretary of Education William J. Bennett said: "This year the news is not what it should be: test scores are in a dead stall."[3]

Test scores in the U.S. also look disappointing when compared to scores in other countries. In a 1983 international comparison of eighth grade test scores in the U.S. with those of other industrialized countries, the National Commission for Excellence in Education found the U.S. ranked twelfth of fourteen countries. When algebra and calculus scores of high school seniors in the top 5 percent of their classes were compared, students in the U.S. ranked last among students from twelve countries.[4]

As we look more closely at test score data, we find that there is a significant difference between the scores obtained by children enrolled in public schools and those enrolled in private schools. Two-year average achievement growth by students in Catholic schools is an additional 0.9 to 1.8 grade equivalents beyond the two-year equivalents gained in the public schools. Other private school students achieve 0.6 to 2.0 grade equivalents greater.[5] In other words, over the course of one school year,

21

Performance by 8th Grade Students in Mathematics Test, 1982

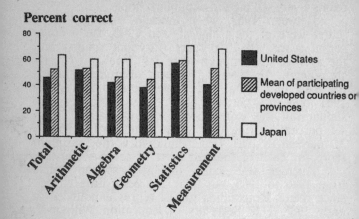

Percent correct

United States

Mean of participating developed countries or provinces

Japan

Performance by 12th Grade Advanced Mathematics Students, 1982

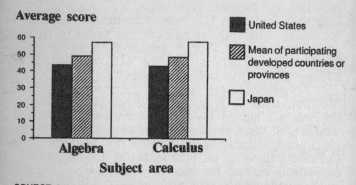

Average score

United States

Mean of participating developed countries or provinces

Japan

Subject area

SOURCE: International Association for the Evaluation of Educational Achievement, Second International Mathematics Study, 1986 reports.

students in Catholic schools increase their learning from 45 percent to 90 percent more than their public school counterparts, and other private school students are learning from 30 percent to 100 percent more.

After controlling for family background, studies show students in Catholic schools still do better than those in public schools, but the difference is less: 0.2 to 0.9 grade equivalents. Students in other private schools perform unevenly when family background is controlled: change in average test scores ranges from -0.7 grade equivalents in mathematics to +1.2 grades for reading. The enhanced performance of students in Catholic schools is true for children of both high and low achievement.[6]

What do all these numbers mean? Very simply, they mean that the average child in the U.S. today is learning less in school than he did ten or twenty years ago. They also mean that this problem is not afflicting other major industrial countries. And finally, they mean this problem is particularly serious in the *public* schools.

Test scores are, to be sure, an incomplete measure of all the tangible and intangible outcomes of schooling. But even those who place little stock in such tests must admit that groups with ultimate legal responsibility for public education -- legislatures and state and local school boards -- have increasingly come to evaluate the outcomes of schooling by means of scores on national or locally designed achievement tests. Whether educators desire it or not, governors, legislators, citizens, and parents are demanding measurable achievement comparisons.[7] And, judging by the numbers, the public schools are failing to produce satisfactory results.

Dropout Rates

Nationwide, the average dropout rate for public schools is 27 percent.[8] This rate varies dramatically depending on a number of factors. Large urban areas, for example, typically have higher dropout rates: New York has a projected dropout rate of 41.6 percent; Miami, 29.5 percent; and Chicago, between 42.8 percent and 53 percent.[9]

Dropout rates also vary by ethnic group. The national average dropout rate for sophomores in the class of 1980 was 13.7 percent for whites, 21.6 percent for blacks, and 27.1 percent for Hispanics.[10] The disparity among ethnic groups is largest in urban areas, with Miami, Detroit, and Chicago all reporting substantially higher dropout rates for blacks and Hispanics than for whites.[11]

As in the case of test scores, a significant difference in dropout rates exists between public and nonpublic schools. Looking only at the probability of dropping out of school between the start of the sophomore year and the start of the senior year, researchers have found an average dropout rate for public schools of 14.4 percent, 3.4 percent for Catholic schools, and 11.9 percent for other private schools.[12]

Spending Levels

Spending on public schools has been increasing rapidly in recent years. Between the 1969-70 and 1985-86 school years, spending per pupil nationwide increased 351 percent in current dollars. After adjusting for inflation, the increase was 56 percent.[13] Spending per pupil remained relatively unchanged between 1977-78 and 1981-82, but rose rapidly during the next three years.[14]

Spending for schools in the U.S. is also high when compared to spending in other countries. The U.S. spends about 6.7 percent of its gross national product on education, compared with 5.7 percent in Japan and 4.5 percent for West Germany. Significantly, Japan produces educational results that are consistently and dramatically better than those of

24

Trends in Public School Spending (Per Pupil)

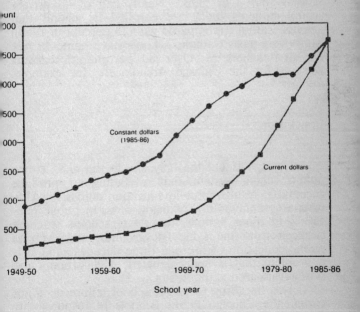

School year

Constant dollars (1985-86)

Current dollars

SOURCE: Center for Education Statistics, *Statistics of State School Systems, Revenues and Expenditures for Public Elementary and Secondary Education*, "Common Core of Data" survey, and unpublished tabulations.

25

our own, better funded, schools. (West Germany does not participate in international surveys of educational performance.) At 18 percent, the U.S. spends a larger portion of its total tax dollars on education than any other country recently surveyed by the United Nations.[15] Moreover, this percentage is considerably higher than those in the next two highest ranking countries, Norway and Sweden.

Closer to home, we can compare spending on public schools to the amount spent on comparable education at private schools. Public schools spend, on average, about $4,000 per pupil per year. The average private school in the U.S. spends only $2,500, and the average Catholic school spends a mere $1,400. The reason private schools can get by so cheaply is *not* that they tend to be Catholic schools staffed by nuns. Nearly half of all private school students today are enrolled in schools that are not Catholic (compared with 13 percent in 1965). Moreover, most Catholic schools have come to rely on lay teachers.[16] Over 80 percent of teachers working for the Chicago Archdiocese, for example, are lay.[17]

Conclusion

Chicago is not the only city in the U.S. with a public school system that is failing to produce acceptable results. Public education across the U.S. compares unfavorably, in many ways, to public education in other nations, to private schools teaching children from the same backgrounds, and even to public education of two and three decades ago. It is a problem that is being debated in classrooms and statehouses around the nation.

This backdrop of public school failure does not excuse the Chicago Public Schools of responsibility for their failure, since by almost every measure the failure in Chicago is worse than it is in other parts of the country. But it does raise the possibility that public schools in Chicago and the rest of the nation are failing for some of the same reasons. Chicago's schools may be experiencing the symptoms of a disease that has not yet reached so advanced a state elsewhere in the nation.

In the next chapter we look beyond test scores and dropout rates to a problem that is more difficult to quantify but is nonetheless of great importance to many parents. That problem is how course content and teaching methods are selected for a public school.

Notes

1. Precisely what falling test scores tell us is a subject of academic debate. More students are taking the tests today, changing the composition of the testing population. As more high-risk students apply for college admission, and hence take standardized tests, their lower test scores have brought down the overall averages.

2. Eileen M. Gardner, "Back to Basics for Black Education" (Washington, D.C.: Heritage Foundation "Critical Issues" series, 1987). Ms. Gardner cites Congressional Budget Office figures from April 1986.

3. William J. Bennett, Statement of February 25, 1988 (Washington, D.C.: U.S. Dept. of Education, 1988).

4. U.S. Dept. of Education, *A Nation At Risk* (1983) and *What Works* (1986), pp. 28, 30.

5. James S. Coleman and Thomas Hoffer, *Public and Private High Schools: The Impact of Communities* (New York: Basic Books, 1987), pp. 66-68.

6. Ibid., p. 78.

7. National Governors Association, *A Time For Results*, 1986; Herbert J. Walberg and J.W. Keefe, *Rethinking Reform: The Principal's Dilemma* (Reston, VA: National Association of Secondary School Principals, 1987).

8. Designs for Change, *The Bottom Line: Chicago's Failing Schools and How to Save Them* (Chicago, January 1985), p. 9.

9. Floyd Morgan Hammack, "Large School Systems' Dropout Reports: An Analysis of Definitions, Procedures and Findings," Spring 1986, pp. 330-334. The higher estimate for the Chicago public school dropout rate comes from Designs for Change, ibid.

10. U.S. Dept. of Education, Center for Education Statistics, *The Condition of Education: A Statistical Report*, 1987 Edition, p. 28. The U.S. Department of Education's "High School and Beyond" project has found that nearly 40 percent of the dropouts returned by 1984 to complete their high school education.

11. Hammack, pp. 330, 334-5; National Commission on Secondary Education for Hispanics, *Make Something Happen*, 1984, p. 23.

12. Coleman and Hoffer, p. 99.

13. U.S. Department of Education, *Elementary and Secondary Education Indicators in Brief*, 1987, p. 22.

14. U.S. Dept. of Education, *The Condition of Education*, p. 35.

15. Ibid., pp. 16-17.

16. "Today Catholic schools enroll 56 percent of all private school students, down from 87 percent in 1965. Other religiously affiliated schools enroll 24 percent of all private school students, compared with 8 percent in 1965. Non-religiously affiliated schools [have] 20 percent of private school enrollment today compared with 5 percent two decades ago." Emily Feistritzer, National Center for Education Information, Washington, DC., *Wall Street Journal*, December 1, 1987.

17. Chicago Archdiocese, *Chicago Catholic Schools*, 1987-88 Report.

3

THE BATTLE OVER CURRICULUM

Textbook writing has . . . become an extension of broader political battles. From evangelical and pentecostal organizations come demands to endorse creationism and an absolute set of traditional values; more secularized conservatives may seek textbooks that glorify private associations, free markets, and patriotism. From globalists, statists, environmentalists, and relativists of one stripe or another come demands for new political and cultural catechisms, militantly secular and often anti-capitalist and anti-nationalist. Pressure that focuses on more narrow interests comes from ethnic groups, feminists, sex educators, church/state separatists, nuclear disarmers, and a host of others.

Gilbert T. Sewall
Phi Delta Kappan
April 19, 1988

Even when a public school system yields test scores and dropout rates that compare favorably with those of other school systems, nationally or internationally, many parents are still disappointed with the education their children receive. This is because curriculum decisions are often made without parental or community participation.

Many parents sense an injustice when they are compelled to support schools that promote views and values at odds with their own. This sense of injustice is magnified when parents and community members are excluded from the process that determines curricula, and when they are not allowed to enroll their children in other schools that better reflect their views. When these parents represent minority or unpopular views in their communities, we must ask whether it is acceptable for public schools to be used by a cultural majority to impose its customs and beliefs on minorities. When the dissatisfied parents are a majority of all parents, we should ask whether better-educated elites should be able to overrule parents and impose (or forbid) curricula that parents oppose (or support). Clearly these are not simple matters.

In this chapter we examine how curriculum decisions are made and explain why the issue is so important in Chicago and other school systems across the country. In later chapters we will discuss how programs that include parental and community involvement in curricula decisions could address these problems.

Who Controls Curricula?

Control over school curricula in the Chicago Public Schools has fluctuated between the Department of Curriculum at the central office and school-based principals and teachers. A survey of the school system in 1964, for example, found that the formal policy of having all curriculum planning done by the central office was routinely circumvented in practice by classroom teachers.[1] Former superintendent of schools Ruth Love centralized control over curricula when she implemented a mastery learning program in the early 1980s, but the program was discontinued when Manford Byrd, Jr., assumed office in 1985. Byrd has allowed principals and teachers to exercise more control over the curriculum of each school.

In the Chicago Public Schools today, principals and teachers work with consultants from the central office to attempt to establish curricula that meet the particular needs of each school and the learning objectives and mandates established by the state and the Board of Education. Standardized tests are used to ensure that systemwide objectives are being reached. Parents and other community members who are members of the local school improvement councils may offer advice on curricula to principals, but the principals are not required to follow their advice. Moreover, since principals ultimately report to (and often seek promotion to) the central office, parents and community members on the councils have even less influence over decisions.

If local school improvement councils had greater authority over curricula, it nevertheless would be difficult for teachers and principals to accommodate the wishes of individual parents. The average public elementary school in Chicago has an enrollment of six hundred students; the average high school enrolls 1,790.[2] These schools are large in comparison with nonpublic schools in the Chicago area as well as with typical public schools downstate. For example, enrollment in the average Catholic elementary school is 60 percent, and in Catholic high schools just 40 percent, of the public school averages.[3] The total enrollment -- elementary as well as high school -- of an average school district in downstate Illinois is less than the enrollment of a single high school in Chicago.

Such large schools mean that the views of each parent necessarily are less likely to influence school policy. The parents of a child enrolled in a typical high school, for example, must compete for the attention of the school principal with the parents of nearly two thousand other students.

Elsewhere in the country, the challenge of accommodating diverse views has been growing with the size of the average school district. In 1930, the average school board member in the United States represented about 250 citizens. In 1972, a school board member had to represent over *two thousand* concerned parents and community members.[4] Not surprisingly, this increase in the scale of public schooling has resulted in unresponsiveness to individual parents and community members.

In school districts where the student population is largely homogeneous, parents are more likely to agree with one another, so the lack of influence by individual parents is likely to cause less parental dissatisfaction. But in districts with many different ethnic, cultural, and religious minorities, almost any curriculum adopted by a school is likely to violate the values and beliefs of at least some parents. In very large districts such as Chicago, then, the size of the schools can be a major source of dissatisfaction.

Where control over curricula has devolved to the school level, parental dissatisfaction can be reduced if parents are allowed to select the public school with the curriculum that most closely matches their interests. Magnet schools and special emphasis schools in Chicago do this only to a limited extent, and are often a true option only for nonminority children or those with sophisticated parents.[5] Most children are required to attend the school to which they are assigned, based on where their families live.

The Chicago Public Schools illustrate three structural factors that bar parental involvement in curricula decisions almost everywhere in America: a decision-making process that formally or informally excludes parents and community members, large-scale districts and schools with large enrollments, and geographic assignment of students to neighborhood schools. Parents in Chicago and across the country are becoming increasingly vocal about their dissatisfaction with the content of their public schools.

Measuring Parental Dissatisfaction

By a margin of almost six to one, Americans feel that parents of public school students should have more say, rather than less say, in deciding which courses are offered by their schools. The margin grows to ten to one among public school parents surveyed, and all the way to sixteen to one among parents who have chosen not to send their children to public schools. Similarly, large majorities of parents and the general public believe parents of public school students should have greater say rather than less say in the selection of instructional materials and books placed in school libraries.[6]

Surveys also show that a large majority (75 percent) of Americans feel that students should be required to take more courses "in basic subjects, such as math and science, thus reducing the amount of elective courses students can take."[7] Strong support for expanding course requirements was also found in a 1985 survey of Chicagoans, with black respondents preferring more course requirements than either Hispanic or white respondents.[8]

Additional evidence of parental dissatisfaction was uncovered in 1984, when the United States Department of Education conducted public hearings across the country on federal regulations intended to protect students from exposure to forms of school instruction their parents might find objectionable.[9] These hearings elicited thirteen hundred pages of testimony from scores of parents, students, teachers, and community leaders describing their negative experiences with curricula and personnel in public school systems throughout the nation. The hearings revealed that parental and community dissatisfaction with the specific content of public education can run very deep, regardless of the academic performance of particular schools. Concerns most commonly raised fit into five categories:

Parental Authority. Many witnesses testified that they perceived their schools to be systematically breaking the bond of authority between parents and their children. A woman in Pittsburgh, Pennsylvania, for example, complained of a curriculum she believed was designed "to create tensions and conflict between parents and their children by having the students regard parents as old-fashioned, unlearned in the ways of the world, and, therefore, unfit to guide and direct them."[10]

Traditional Ethics and Culture. Parents voiced their opposition to certain curricula that called into question even their most basic convictions about right and wrong, and about traditional family roles. A mother in Milwaukie, Oregon said her son participated for two years without his parents' knowledge or consent in a curriculum that represented "a deliberate attempt to manipulate and indoctrinate our children into a philosophical belief that morals and ethics are relative." Her son "came home one day very confused as to the rightness or wrongness of stealing from a store."[11]

Sexual Morality. Parents and teachers repeatedly complained about the messages children were receiving in public schools about sexual behavior and attitudes. For example, a teacher testified in Kansas City, Missouri that the library at his elementary school was circulating a short film in which "out of six minutes, there were three minutes of a spread crotch shot of a man exposing . . . his male organs. I do not think that there is a place in elementary school libraries for such material to be viewed by nine- and ten-year-olds."[12]

Religious Views. While much of the commentary on religion and public education over the last thirty years has emphasized the legal and ethical imperative of official neutrality in the classroom, it is clear some parents believe that mandate is being ignored by those hostile to traditional religious views. In Kansas City, Missouri a teacher testified that a guidance counselor had told his students in a classroom session, "'Christianity once served our country in a positive way, but now students today should seek other forms of religion to study and learn from. . .'. Then the counselor suggested yoga and meditation, and some of the eastern mystic religions."[13]

Political Views. A parent from Wolfeboro, New Hampshire complained about an activist group that allegedly conducted "a classroom discussion of nuclear weapons, war and atomic holocaust for second, third and fourth grade students. . . . One of the nine year olds said it was so scary that she felt 'like I should just cut my head off.'"[14]

These samples reflect the tone of the 1984 hearings. Yet anger over the substance of public education has by no means been confined to traditionalists. In 1973, then-Senator Walter Mondale held hearings on the Women's Educational Equity Act, which he sponsored. In the hearings, witnesses complained of systematic sexism in the public school textbooks and curricula. As one testified:

> From the time a young girl enters school she learns more than just reading, writing, and arithmetic. Her textbooks are far more likely to be written about boys and men; girls and women are rarely major characters. She will read about boys who do interesting, exciting things; they build rafts and treehouses; they have challenging adventures and solve problems, and they rescue girls who are "so stupid" that they get into trouble. One typical book pictures a fourteen-year-old girl standing on

37

a chair, screaming because there is a frog on the floor; her eight-year-old brother rescues her.[15]

Despite their differences in tone, both the 1984 and the 1973 hearings reflected the deep concern of parents, teachers, and community members over the content of public school education. This concern spans political and ideological differences; it pervades public schooling across the nation. Yet there is a paradox: though a majority of parents are united by their desire for more, rather than less, parental direction over the substance of public education, they are deeply divided over what that content should be. Three national controversies illustrating the depth of these divisions concern creationism, sex education, and instructional methods.

Clashes in the Science Classroom

Science instruction in public schools has changed dramatically from the period before 1925, when teaching the theory of evolution was forbidden in some states because of its challenge to the Biblical account of creation. Today, the federal courts have declared that teaching natural history theories compatible with or based upon the Biblical account violate the establishment clause of the Constitution. The issue remains unsettled.

Creationists assert that science *per se* can provide no ultimate certainty about origins because its method simply assumes the historic uniformity and continuity of observed natural cycles and inferred laws. Their catastrophist model of natural history, which is compatible with Biblical accounts of instant creation and the Noahic Flood, assumes the possibility of unique and cataclysmic events in the geological past, about which inferences from observed natural processes and rates today tell us little or nothing.   Creationists believe that exclusive presentation of evolutionary theory in public classrooms amounts to unscientific dogmatism, and tacit state establishment of a religion of materialist atheism.

Evolutionists, with most of the public education and scientific communities on their side, argue that creationist theory is merely a pseudo-scientific recapitulation of Genesis, and that its advocates assume the existence of an intervening divine hand with the capacity to alter natural processes in the world.   Allowing creationism to be portrayed as a scientific theory in public classrooms would be to confuse theological speculation with the careful rigor and methodology of the physical sciences.   To promote such ideas in the public classroom, they say, would constitute an establishment of traditional religion.

The Louisiana legislature accepted the arguments of creationists in 1982, passing a law requiring that evolutionary theory and creationism be presented as equally legitimate, but ultimately unprovable, theories in public school curricula.   The argument of evolutionists, however, has prevailed in the federal courts.

Each view has adherents among public school parents and teachers. In Illinois a public school teacher in Will County's New Lenox School District has filed suit in federal court arguing that his Constitutional rights have been violated by an administrator who has prohibited him from teaching creationism.[16]   In 1987, three individuals ran for election to Wheaton's School Board on creationist platforms, without success.

The point here is not that one side is right and the other wrong, but that these groups face a "winners-take-all" battle in the public schools as they currently are structured.

The same kind of heated disagreement takes place over the teaching of sex education. As was evident in the 1984 hearings quoted above, some parents and teachers regard much of the content of sex education in public schools as morally skewed and hostile to their more traditional perspectives. Such opinions have also been expressed in Chicago.

A mother of six who has had her children in Chicago, suburban, and now private school settings recently said she "could not tolerate the product or priorities of the public schools." At Walt Disney Magnet School in Chicago, she said, "my four-year-old daughter was being taught sex education before she was being taught to read."[17]

In 1986, a group of South Side parents, students, and Protestant ministers filed suit to halt distribution of contraceptives by health clinics in public schools. Among the defendants are the Chicago Board of Education and the Illinois Department of Public Health, which respectively accommodate and finance the operation of contraceptive-distributing clinics in Chicago's DuSable, Orr, and Crane high schools. The plaintiffs, mostly black, charge that the practice undermines parental authority and represents a "pernicious effort to destroy the very fabric of family life among black parents and their children."[18]

The Illinois legislature voted in 1987 to ban contraceptive distribution and abortion counseling in public schools, but the bill was vetoed by Governor James R. Thompson. Legislators who supported the bill did so in part out of their conviction that parents, not public schools, should instruct children in matters of sexual behavior. Yet many of these same Illinois lawmakers voted to enact a law in 1987 mandating public school instruction statewide on the merits of sexual abstinence until marriage.

Such apparent contradictions suggest that much conflict could be avoided if the public schools simply refrained from teaching controversial topics. But even if the curricula of public schools were radically reduced to reading, writing, and arithmetic, parental dissatisfaction would remain. The recent history of public education is filled with controversies over instructional methods.

Instructional Methods

During the open classroom movement of the early 1970s, advocates such as Charles Silberman criticized classroom "preoccupation with order and control, the slavish adherence to the timetable and lesson plan, the obsession with routine qua routine, the absence of noise and movement, . . . the formal lecture or teacher-dominated 'discussion' in which the teacher instructs the entire class as a unit."[19] Advocates of basic education, on the other hand, regard many of these elements -- without Silberman's pejoratives -- as essential to learning.

Public school children, parents, and teachers of the last three decades have been caught up in similar pedagogical storms stirred by proponents of the new math and defenders of traditional mathematics teaching. Similarly, this generation has been whipsawed between advocates of traditional phonics and those promoting "look-say" sight reading. In Chicago, school administrators echoed education theorists in defense of an unpopular 1988 Board of Education decision to spend thousands of dollars on handheld calculators for a student population unable to compute with pencil and paper.

It is not only parents who are divided over issues of technique. Professor Diane Ravitch recently cited with incredulity a headline in *Education Week*: "Using 'Real Books' to Teach Reading Said to Heighten Skill, Interest." The news in the article, said Ravitch, was a school experiment in which children learning to read with storybooks appeared to enjoy reading more than those practicing with basal readers. These children were reported in later years to be superior writers. Ravitch asks:

> Is it now "experimental" and "innovative" to propose that young children should read good literature and that it might be more enjoyable than a basal reader? Is it possible that America's reading teachers think a controlled vocabulary "developed" by pedestrian writers can compete with the works of the Brothers Grimm, Hans Christian Anderson, L. Frank Baum, or the *Myths of Many Lands*?[20]

The point is not to judge one pedagogical practice better than another, but to demonstrate that even the most basic school subjects -- reading, writing, and arithmetic -- can be the focus of furious disagreement among and within each of the major groups controlling the content of public education: parents, teachers, administrators, and theorists.

Conclusion

Would we, as parents, be happy to enroll our children in the Chicago Public Schools (or any other public school system) if other students in the system were reading and computing as well as the best students in the nation? Perhaps some of us would, but others would not. The local public schools to which our children would be assigned could still be teaching a curriculum that is at odds with our personal beliefs and values. We still would be excluded from the process in which curriculum decisions are made, and we still would not be allowed to move our child to another public school in hopes of finding a different teacher or principal who might be sympathetic to our beliefs.

The Chicago Public Schools do not give the public a voice in determining school curricula. Because the average school's enrollment is so large, and because students are assigned to schools based on where their families live, it is inevitable that many parents will be disappointed with the content of the education their children receive.

During the past three years, the Chicago Public Schools have moved in the direction of school-based control over curricula. This trend has placed greater authority in the hands of principals and classroom teachers who are more likely to understand the specific needs and interests of their communities. Certainly this progress is to be cheered.

But the trend toward school-based curriculum decisions has excluded parents and community members. The challenge is to find a role for them.

1. Robert J. Havighurst, *The Public Schools of Chicago* (Chicago: Board of Education of the City of Chicago, 1964). A survey of over three hundred classroom teachers and about one hundred elementary and high school principals found "a great range" in the use of curriculum guides prepared by the central office. "Some teachers use the guides for the subjects in which they feel the least competent. Some do not use them at all. Some teachers use the guides because they feel they have to." (p. 97).

2. Chicago Panel on Public School Policy and Finance, *Who Benefits from Desegregation?* (Chicago, December 1987). Figures are for 1985-86 school year.

3. Archdiocese of Chicago, *Chicago Catholic Schools*, 1987-88 Edition.

4. J.W. Guthrie, "Organization Scale and School Success," *Educational Evaluation and Policy Analysis*, Vol. 1, No. 1 (1979), pp. 17, 27.

5. "Not only did the magnet schools 'cream off' the most ambitious students (or those with the most ambitious parents) they received more financial resources than schools whose students were supposed to receive extra resources to compensate for remaining racially isolated." Chicago Panel on Public School Finances, *Who Benefits From Desegregation?* p. 43.

6. Alec M. Gallup and David L. Clark, "The 1987 Phi Delta Kappa/Gallup Poll of the Public's Attitudes Toward the Public Schools," *Phi Delta Kappan*, September 1987, p. 21.

7. Ibid.

8. Herbert J. Walberg and G. Alfred Hess, Jr., *Chicagoans View Their Public Schools* (Chicago: Chicago Panel On Public School Finances, June 1985).

9.   U.S. Department of Education, "Official Transcript of Proceedings in the Matter of the Proposed Regulations to Implement the Protection of Pupil Rights Amendment (Section 439 of the General Education Provisions Act, 20 U.S. Code S1232h), Also Known as the Hatch Amendment."

10. Ibid., Hearings of March 16, 1984, Pittsburgh, Pennsylvania.

11. Ibid., Hearings of March 13, 1984, Seattle, Washington.

12. Ibid., Hearings of March 19, 1984, Kansas City, Missouri.

13. Ibid.

14. Ibid., Hearings of March 21, 1984, Concord, New Hampshire.

15. U.S. Congress, Senate Subcommittee on Education of the Committee on Labor and Public Welfare, *Women's Educational Equity Act of 1973*, 93d Congress, Second Session, 1973, pp. 393-396.

16. *Chicago Tribune*, March 22, 1988.

17. Statement of Jan Arduini, spokesperson for Christian Home Educators Coalition, released at a Springfield, Illinois press conference on April 14, 1988. Reported in *The Daily Herald*, April 15, 1988.

18. *Chicago Tribune*, October 16, 1986.

19. Quoted by Diane Ravitch, *The Troubled Crusade* (New York: Basic Books, 1983), p. 247.

20. Diane Ravitch, *The Schools We Deserve* (New York: Basic Books, 1985), pp. 76-77.

PART TWO

WHY THE CHICAGO PUBLIC SCHOOLS DO NOT WORK

4

HOW THE CHICAGO PUBLIC SCHOOLS BECAME CENTRALIZED

Schools in American cities may yet be paying the price for the successes of turn-of-the-century reform. The highly structured educational systems which emerged from that period remain essentially intact, increasing the difficulty of evolving programs and institutions relevant to the demands and needs of a constantly changing urban society and frequently impeding the flow of communications between the schools themselves and the public they serve.

William Bullough
*Cities and Schools
in the Gilded Age*

One of the most prominent characteristics of the Chicago Public Schools is the degree to which management is centralized. A single board of education -- whose members are appointed, not elected -- runs an enterprise with annual revenues of nearly $2 billion. Over three thousand administrators staff central and regional offices. Parental involvement in decision making at the school level is nonexistent or largely illusory. Even principals and school teachers have limited authority over the day-to-day operation of their schools and classrooms.

Why was this kind of organization chosen for the Chicago Public Schools? The answer has to do with the rise of public education itself, and the rationales and justifications that led to its widespread acceptance.

Public schools, or "common" schools as they were once called, were heavily influenced by a nationalist campaign to promote a common language, a common set of values, and a loyalty to the institutions of government rather than to church and family. Advocates of public schools believed these goals could best be met by school systems that were centralized and resistant to parental involvement. This organizational form, probably inappropriate even for its time but now certainly so, continues to exist in Chicago.

Before Public Schools

The first school in America, founded in 1635, was tax funded.[1] It was the Boston Latin School, in Boston, Massachussets. Tax-supported schools opened soon afterwards in Charlestown and Dorchester. Though publicly financed, these schools were much different from what we now know as public schools. Existing in intensely religious communities over one hundred years before any Constitutional restriction on government establishment of religion, these schools were tax funded *and* religious. Their curricula reflected the Puritan beliefs of the town founders, with a strong focus on classical languages. Since most instruction was in Latin, the schools came to be called Latin schools.

Early in the eighteenth century, New England's Latin schools came under growing criticism for failing to equip their students with the tools and knowledge needed to succeed in the practical world. Benjamin Franklin, among others, decried the absence of "useful learning" in the public schools and their failure to teach in the vernacular. The Latin schools, they said, were increasingly out of touch with the needs of the great majority of people. They were teaching a curriculum suited to an elite preparing for lives in religious and academic institutions, not the average man preparing for practical business and community affairs.

The Latin schools resisted calls for change for a long time. As a result, private schools, called academies, were begun. The first was the Philadelphia Academy, established in 1751 by Benjamin Franklin. Another, the Phillips Academy, was started in Andover, Massachussets, in 1778. True to Franklin's earlier statements, the new academies taught in the vernacular and emphasized "useful learning," including history, geography, natural and applied sciences, and modern languages.

Soon thousands of academies were operating in communities throughout the United States. In 1855, at least six thousand academies were operating with total enrollment of over 263,000 students.[2] Some of these schools combined public and private control and financing, but most often control was in the hands of private boards of trustees. Gradually, the Latin schools bowed to pressure from the competing academies and began to revamp their curricula. Many, unwilling or unable to change, closed their doors.

During the time that the first public schools gradually were being replaced by private academies, but before the rise of compulsory universal public education in the mid-1800s, most parents in the

51

United States educated their children privately, either at home or in voluntarily funded schools of their choice. This period of over one hundred years of nonpublic education saw a dramatic increase in literacy among all income and ethnic groups in the United States.

Enrollment at the private schools was not limited to the children of the wealthy. Many of the private schools adjusted their tuition to accommodate the income of the parents. Education historian Joel Spring writes:

> [T]he private schools were common in several respects. First, they were the most common or prevalent system of education. Second, they provided what was called a common system of education. And third, they were attended in common by children from a wide range of families with differing incomes and occupations.[3]

Prior to the 1830s, most public schools were "charity schools" formed to take in children from the very poorest families. (Boston was one exception: it had a system of tax supported schools in the 1790s.) These schools were soon pressed into service for the children of new immigrants, and were promoted by some social workers as a solution to the problems of poverty and crime. Though private schools were flourishing and open to children of the less well-off as well as the wealthy, the charity schools were promoted by some as a model for uniform or "common" education for children from all walks of life.

The common school movement began when leading educators adopted the charity school as the model for free and compulsory schooling for all students, regardless of their parents' wealth. As the next section will show, they opted for this model because it allowed widespread adoption of a common curriculum, not because it taught children faster or better, or because it satisfied parents more.

The Call for a "Common" Curriculum

Throughout the nineteenth century, Americans were separated by language, religion, ethnic background, political belief, and a myriad of other aspects of ideology and lifestyle.[4] Nowhere was this more true than in the growing cities of the new nation. In the minds of some people, tolerating this diversity was wrong and even dangerous. Social reformer Jacob Riis, for example, wrote in 1882: "The immediate duty which the community has to perform for its own protection is to school the children first of all into good Americans, and next into useful citizens."[5]

Ellwood Cubberley, an influential educator and historian at the turn of the century, described immigrants of the late nineteenth century as being "illiterate, docile, lacking in initiative, and almost wholly without the Anglo-Saxon conceptions of righteousness, liberty, law, order, public decency, and government." According to Cubberley, these immigrants "served to dilute tremendously our national stock and to weaken and corrupt our political life."[6]

Tax-funded schools were viewed by educators such as Cubberley as a tool for bringing about the speedy assimilation of the new immigrants. Common schools -- tax-supported public schools open to all children, using a common curriculum, and emphasizing the training of citizenship -- were promoted as a way to take from the church and family their traditional roles in the education of children. The intellectual founders of today's public schools repeatedly emphasized that their goal was to impose, from the top down, a single uniform set of values and habits. Only by enforcing this common national curriculum, they argued, could the new nation fulfill its destiny as a great nation.

Noah Webster, an early advocate of tax-funded common schools, wrote: "Good republicans . . . are formed by a singular machinery in the body politic, which takes the child as soon as he can speak, checks his natural independence and passions, makes him subordinate to superior age, to the laws of the state, to town and parochial institutions."[7]   Webster's view of common schools as a means to impose on the nation a uniform set of beliefs extended to political values as well, as is illustrated by the "Federal Catechism" that formed part of his famous *Spelling Book*.[8]

Benjamin Rush, another prominent common school advocate, was even more emphatic in calling for the use of schools to forge new loyalty to the state. He wrote: "Let our pupil be taught that he does not belong to himself, but that he is public property. Let him be taught to love his family, but let him be taught at the same time that he must forsake and even forget them when the welfare of his country requires it."[9]

Horace Mann, a wealthy Massachusetts lawyer and state legislator, was the common schools' strongest advocate for many years. Even today his *12th Annual Report to the Massachusetts Board of Education*, delivered in 1848, is looked to as an essential statement of the purpose and goals of public education. In it, Mann expresses his belief that "education, then, beyond all other devices of human origin, is the great equalizer of the conditions of men-- the balance-wheel of the social machinery." And according to Joel Spring:

> In a sense, Mann's reports represented the official justification for the creation of a common system of education. Involved in this justification was the hope that all the social, economic, and political programs of society would be solved by putting together in a common school the children of all members of society and by teaching them a common set of political and moral beliefs.[10]

In large cities such as Chicago, the new public school systems developed centralized administrative structures that allowed influential elites to set curricula and make important personnel and spending decisions. One reason given at the time was that education, like manufacturing, could become more efficient through consolidation and utilization of mass production techniques. But a more important reason was that a centralized school system was better able to prevent immigrants and unpopular ethnic and cultural minorities from participating in the decision-making process.

Recent immigrants were not fluent in the language and often did not understand the organization of American school systems. Moreover, they often brought with them political, social, and religious beliefs that were at odds with the beliefs of the Protestant majority. Allowing these persons to influence the curricula of the public schools would have meant breaking away from the goal of a single national curriculum. It would have meant that "republican" ideas would not always be taught, or that obedience to employers and the state would no longer be emphasized during lessons. Joel Spring summarized the situation this way:

> [T]he idea of a local school reflecting the point of view of its particular constituency was antithetical to the basic ideas of the common school movement. Common school reformers did not want schools to offer different courses of instruction but wanted all instruction to be the same in order to achieve the goal of providing a common education to all people. The creation of a system of common schooling required centralization to assure uniformity of practices.[11]

In Chicago, and in many other cities in America, decentralized school systems were deliberately centralized to prevent parents from having a voice in their children's education. School boards that were once representative of the ethnicity and occupations of the school districts over time came to be dominated by upper-income professionals who could afford to campaign for the ever-smaller number of at-large positions, or who won the favor of the mayors who appointed school board members. Local political organizations and unions came to play a larger role in these elections, too, further assuring that control of the schools remained with a power elite.

Centralization in Practice

The national trend toward larger districts and less decentralized decision making has continued to this day. It is reflected by the dramatic increase in the number of students enrolled in an average public school district, from just two hundred in 1930 to almost three thousand in 1972.[12] As a result of this consolidation, the average number of citizens represented by each school board member has also risen dramatically, from about 250 in 1930 to over two thousand in 1972.[13]

Recent research on the effects of school district consolidation lays to rest the myth that education can benefit from organizational forms designed for mass production. Studies repeatedly show that bigger districts yield lower student achievement and poorer student, parent, and staff morale.[14] Studies have also found that larger districts produce acceptable outcomes less efficiently than do smaller districts.[15] Comprehensive studies taking into account socioeconomic status also show an inverse relationship between the size of district enrollment and learning.[16]

The educational blight of Detroit, Los Angeles, New York, and other large cities is well known, yet their per-student expenditure levels are often considerably higher than the average of surrounding, smaller, suburban districts. A recent study of school district size in New York State, for example, concluded that "scale economies enjoyed by larger districts can come at the expense of the efficient production of educational outcomes. . . . [E]mpirical evidence from New York State . . . shows that lower levels of efficiency exist in large as compared to small districts."[17]

It is important to note that while district size is inversely related to various measures of learning and educational performance, the evidence does not show that larger districts necessarily spend more per pupil. Very small districts (say, those with fewer than three hundred students and especially those with fewer than two hundred) spend more per student than do larger districts. This is caused in part by the need for a school board, superintendent, principal, and some minimum staff and equipment regardless of how small the district is. Also contributing to the higher cost are the higher transportation costs of low-enrollment districts, which are likely to be in sparsely populated areas. The per-pupil costs of districts with between five hundred and five thousand or more students, however, differ very little.[18] The trend toward larger districts, then, may contribute to poor achievement but not to higher costs per pupil.

Conclusion

The modern public school is the product of an ideological movement of the late nineteenth and early twentieth centuries. That movement sought to give the state power to impose a common set of values and skills on a heterogeneous population. Centralized administration of large city school systems was used as a way to insulate public school curriculum decisions from parents and other com-

57

munity members whose values and traditions were at odds with what was taught in the schools.

Many people are now questioning whether this goal is desirable and whether the management system designed to implement the goal can respond to the new concerns and demands of a large city in the twentieth century. Large majorities of Americans, as we saw in Chapter Three, favor giving parents a stronger role in determining curricula. Moreover, as we will see in the following chapters, there is evidence that this centralized management structure has given rise to many of the other problems that affect the Chicago Public Schools and public schools across the country.

1. This history of early public schools in the United States is taken largely from four sources: Joel Spring, *The American School, 1642 - 1985* (White Plains, NY: Longman, Inc., 1986); Carl Kaestle, *Pillars of the Republic: Common Schools and American Society, 1780-1860* (New York: Hill and Wang, 1983); Murray N. Rothbard, *Education, Free and Compulsory* (Wichita, KS: Center for Independent Education, 1979); and "History of Education," *Encyclopedia Britannica*, 15th ed (1979), Vol. 6, pp. 316-408.
2. Spring, p. 19.
3. Ibid., p. 52.
4. This history of common schools is taken from several sources including "The Evolving Political Structure of American Schooling," by Joel Spring, "Nineteenth-Century Opponents of State Education," by George H. Smith, and "Schooling for Work and Working at School," by C.H. Edson, all in *The Public School Monopoly*, edited by Robert B. Everhart (San Francisco: Pacific Institute for Public Policy Research, 1982); Joel Spring, *The American School, 1642-1985*; and David Tyack, *The One Best System* (Cambridge, MA: Harvard University Press, 1974).
5. Everhart, p. 163.
6. Quoted in Everhart, p. 164.
7. Ibid., p. 82.
8. Spring, p. 38.
9. Everhart, p. 83.
10. Spring, p. 89.
11. Ibid., p. 100.
12. Figures are for the mean. J.W. Guthrie, "Organization Scale and School Success," *Educational Evaluation and Policy Analysis*, Vol. 1, No. 1 (1979), pp. 17-27.

13. Ibid. The number of school districts in the United States fell from 127,531 in 1931-32 to 15,734 in 1986-87. *Digest of Educational Statistics* (U.S. Department of Education, Center for Education Statistics, 1988), p. 29; *Directory of Public Elementary and Secondary Education Agencies*, Fall 1986, p. xii.

14. Ibid.; see also W.F. Fox, "Reviewing Economies of Size in Education," *Journal of Educational Finance*, Vol. 6, Winter 1981, pp. 273-296; R. J. Butler and D.H. Monk, "The Cost of Public Schooling in New York State: The Role of Scale and Efficiency in 1978-9," *The Journal of Human Resources*, Vol. 20 (1985), pp. 3-38.

15. C.E. Bidwell and J.D. Kasarda, "School District Organization and Student Achievement," *American Sociological Review*, Vol. 40 (1975), pp. 55-70; R. Turner, G. Camilli, R. Kroc, and J. Hoover, "Policy Strategies, Teacher Salary Incentive, and Student Achievement: An Explanatory Model," *Educational Researcher*, Vol. 15 #3 (1986), pp. 5-11.

16. Herbert J. Walberg and William J. Fowler, Jr., "Expenditure and Size Efficiencies of Public School Districts," *Educational Researcher*, October 1987, pp. 5-13.

17. Butler and Monk, p. 3.

18. Turner, Camilli, Kroc, and Hoover, p. 8.

5

HOW THE CHICAGO PUBLIC SCHOOLS DECLINED

Education has not had to innovate in order to survive. People in business may not welcome competition, but they accept the reality of it. So increasingly they assume the need for change. People in education have not been similarly exposed to competition -- to the risk of failure. So like any managers comfortable in a cartel, they cling tightly to the traditional "givens" of their system.

Ted Kolderie
University of Minnesota

The decline of the Chicago Public Schools can be traced to three factors: barriers to parental involvement, the growth of a huge bureaucracy, and the absence of accountability to the community. These factors interact and feed one another, creating a destructive cycle that frustrates those who would seek to improve the system from the inside. Parents and concerned citizens who realize they have little or no say in how the schools are operated have withdrawn from the process, depriving the schools of the benefits of their active support.

The centralization of school administration discussed in the last chapter is in large part responsible for the barriers to parental involvement in the schools. Though the original rationale for this centralization now has few public supporters, the interest groups that sprang out of the centralization process continue to benefit from it and resist calls for change.

The growth of bureaucracy in the school system can be explained by its missing "bottom line," perverse incentive structures, and the superior organizing abilities of public employees. Almost all public enterprises face the challenge of operating efficiently despite these problems; the Chicago Public Schools have faced this challenge and lost.

The third factor, absence of accountability, arose largely from the practice of geographic assignment of students to schools. Because parents are not allowed to send their children to the public school of their choice, there is no competition among the schools for students or funding. Moreover, since parents who choose to enroll their children in private schools must continue to pay taxes to the public schools, there is little direct competition between public schools and private schools.

Some combination of these three factors, in various stages of development, is probably working to undermine the quality of public schools in almost every town and city in the United States. In Chicago, these factors have caused a state of crisis.

The Importance of Parental Involvement

Parental and community involvement in the learning process have been found repeatedly to improve the educational performance of students.[1] In particular, deliberate cooperative efforts by parents and educators to modify academic conditions in the home have an outstanding record of success in promoting achievement. In twenty-nine controlled studies of the past decade, 91 percent of the comparisons favored children in such programs over nonparticipating children. The average measurable effect of these parental involvement programs was *twice* that of socioeconomic status, and some programs had effects that were *ten times* as large. Since few of the programs lasted more than a semester, the potential for programs providing sustained parental involvement is great.[2]

Observation also supports the view that effective schools are typically those with active and supportive parents. Schools that are successful are almost always characterized by a high level of participation by parents and community members. This participation can take many forms, including classroom help, paper grading, field trips, "homework contracts," and management assistance. The presence or absence of motivated parents can determine the success or failure of a school.

Centralization and Parental Involvement

Centralization of the Chicago Public Schools has closed off many avenues for parental involvement in the schools. Parents can complain or make suggestions to principals in the Chicago Public Schools, but the principals lack many of the powers needed to respond. Principals have little say in the hiring and firing of teachers, supervision of janitors and clerks in their buildings, how the budget for their school is set, and how their building is used outside normal school hours.[3]

The procedure for removing bad teachers is so difficult and time consuming that in 1982 only seven teachers out of 22,825 were dismissed. Teacher dismissal proceedings cost approximately $10,000 and can last for a year or longer.[4] Moreover, most of the waste and featherbedding occurs "upstream" of principals, in the layers of bureaucracy between the individual school and the Board of Education.

The school budgeting process is particularly insulated from community input. In 1987, after sponsoring six hundred public hearings at which more than twelve thousand people submitted testimony, the Chicago Board of Education chose to make no changes at all to its proposed budget.

In 1988, as this book is being written, parents in Chicago are once again expressing their frustration with the barriers erected to keep them from exercising control over their schools. Though state law requires that each public school in the city hold public hearings before approving an annual budget, the parents attending these hearings are given little actual power. Newspaper articles have described a school where just $27,991 of a total budget of $2,385,728 was considered discretionary spending subject to parental advice.[5] Parents do not actually have any say over this tiny allocation, either: school administrators are allowed to change budget allocations after they are approved by parents. Parental approval of budget proposals, in short, is a meaningless gesture.[6]

Parents are also locked out of decisions concerning the selection of courses and instructional materials. As we showed in Chapter 3, parents and community members have a great interest in school curricula, and many support being given a bigger role in the selection of teaching materials and methods. Unfortunately, the local school improvement councils lack any authority over curriculum matters, and the size of many Chicago public schools discourages meaningful participation by parents. Even the last resort of concerned parents, the selection of a public school whose curriculum more closely matches their beliefs, is usually prevented by the Chicago Public Schools. Clearly these barriers to community involvement must make parents and concerned citizens less willing to support the school and assist in the learning process.

PTAs and similar groups also tend to be ineffective because they have only advisory powers. Devoted parents and conscientious principals and teachers can use these forums to discuss issues and improve their schools. But being able to air opinions and talk to teachers is not the same as being able to obtain information or speak with authority on spending or staff matters, and it is the latter that is required if parents are to have an effect on their schools. The difference is crucial, and it is one that many frustrated parents have come to understand.

Bureaucracy and the Missing "Bottom Line"

Next to the barriers to parental involvement in and support of the schools, the largest structural problem facing the Chicago Public Schools is the presence of a large and unresponsive bureaucracy. Why has this bureaucracy been allowed to flourish?

The bureaucracy of the Chicago Public Schools has grown because there is no "bottom line" against which the system's performance can be measured. Without this measurement, inefficient and unnecessary expenditures cannot be separated from efficient and necessary spending. Moreover, individual administrators benefit more from spending increases than from spending reductions (since administrative power and pay are linked to the size of departmental budgets)[7], and they are usually better organized than parents or community representatives.

We can see why the bureaucracy has a natural tendency to grow if we compare the public schools to a private business. In a private business, decisions concerning how much to spend to produce a product are determined by a "bottom line," or profit and loss statement. If we lost money last year, we should either sell a different product or change the way we produce and market last year's product. In either case, we will *spend less* on the activities that failed. The bottom line -- our profit or loss -- is an objective measure of our success or failure at meeting our objective.

In the public schools, our goal would be to run a quality school that parents support. If after one year test scores are falling and disciplinary problems are disrupting classroom activities, we are clearly failing to achieve our goal. But unlike the private business, we do not lose revenues from our "customers" for our failure. Parents are not allowed to withdraw their children from unsatisfactory schools and enroll them in another public school. And removing a child from the public school system altogether is a costly proposition, since the parents must then pay twice for the child's education (through taxes and tuition). Consequently, as administrators of the school we have little fear of losing our "customers" by failing to deliver quality services. The discipline of having a bottom line is lost.

Without a bottom line to consult, we might argue that our failure only shows that *more* money, not less, should be spent next year on our school. Perhaps, we might argue, more people should be hired to study our problems, or to suggest how our programs could be redesigned. The result of failing to perform well, then, could produce a call for *more funding, not less*. Does this sound familiar? It should. Year after year the failure of the Chicago Public Schools has been pointed to as a reason for increasing their funding.

The difference between the private business and the public schools is not that one seeks to make money and the other to provide education. Many schools in Chicago are run as private businesses, and each year they must face the objective test of the bottom line. If a private school cannot raise in tuition and gifts what it spends on staff and overhead, it must eventually close its doors. Its failure to win the support of parents directly leads to insufficient money to operate. Poor performance is punished by decreased revenues, not rewarded by increased funding. This is the discipline of a bottom line.

Bureaucracy and Incentives

Another reason the bureaucracy of the Chicago Public Schools has flourished is that many of its honest and hard-working employees face incentives to act in ways that are not in the best interests of parents and the community. This problem with incentives, like the problem of the missing bottom line, is not unique to the school system. It is a challenge faced by every public institution.

Let us again put ourselves in the shoes of public school administrators. How is our salary determined? Everyone familiar with the Chicago Public Schools knows that the highest salaries are paid to persons who work in the administrative offices, not in the schools. Following standard civil service practices, salaries are usually determined by the size of budget and the number of employees a person manages. As these increase, so do salaries. This means that, as administrators, we will benefit financially if we can justify an increase in the budget we manage or the number of people who report to us.

Faced with the failure of schools to raise test scores, maintain orderly classrooms, or satisfy parents, how would we, as administrators, react? One option would be to cut back funding to person-nel who are failing to produce results, and reward the administrators and teachers at schools who are doing well. But why should we do this? Total income to the schools has stayed the same, despite the poor quality of education produced at some schools. We do not *need* to reduce spending to "balance our budget." Since our salary grows as total spending and employment grow, we will person-ally benefit if we can justify spending more on the ineffective school. Also, since it is much *easier* to keep a bad school open with additional staff and funding than to close the school and reassign (or

67

even dismiss) its staff and relocate its students, we have still another reason to increase funding to the bad school.

The growth of strong unions in public schools across the nation is an illustration of the inappropriate incentives that good people face in a public enterprise. Public school teachers are among the most highly unionized occupations in the U.S.; in 1984, over 72 percent of all public school teachers were covered by collective bargaining agreements negotiated with teachers unions.[8] Managers in public school systems are less likely to resist union organizing or demands than their private-sector counterparts because *their* salaries and careers are unlikely to be affected by unfavorable terms or settlements. Public school managers do not need to take strong stands against employee unions.

These examples make clear the fact that administrators in the public schools face incentives to keep ineffective schools open, and to increase funding in response to failure. This practice translates into an ever-growing budget and bureaucracy, where the response to failure is to spend more and hire more.

Why Parents Are Out-organized

Knowing why bureaucracy is tolerated in the public school system and what propels its growth, we should ask why parents have not organized to resist this trend. As the consumers of an unacceptable product, why have they failed to apply pressure to the schools to reform? This brings us to the third cause of bureaucracy in the Chicago Public Schools: it is much easier to organize teachers, tradesmen, and school administrators than it is to organize parents and taxpayers.

Public school employees are easier to organize because they work together in a single location and therefore can meet regularly and come to know each other. There is little or no cost involved, in lost time or inconvenience, for coworkers to meet and discuss issues of common interest. School employees have many common interests, particularly in assuring job security and increased pay. Since these things are easy to measure and of great personal importance, it is cost effective for public school employees to invest their time in lobbying for more.

Another reason public school employees are so effectively organized is that, as members of the workforce of the largest "business" in the state, public school employees know they form a highly visible and influential voting bloc at the state level. Hearing political candidates make regular appeals for their votes strengthens their self-perception as a group with common interests and considerable influence. The Illinois Education Association, which has 65,000 members, is one of the largest and best-funded lobbying organizations in Illinois.

Compared to public employees, parents and other community members are very difficult to organize. Since they work in different places, many parents see other parents only at special meetings that must take place after working hours, and at a location to which they must travel. The cost, in terms of lost time, travel, and inconvenience, discourages all but the most concerned parents from regularly attending meetings.

Parents also realize that there is less at stake for them than there is for each public school employee. Parents will continue to pay education taxes regardless of what happens at their school, so for them there is no financial reward for participating in the meetings. Moreover, parents realize that the improvements they seek -- a teacher reassigned, more spending on books or supplies, etc. -- are often hard to measure and don't last long. A public school employee facing reassignment, or dismissal if his or her salary is to be rerouted to books or supplies, faces a threat that is very easy to measure and presumably permanent. Clearly the employee will have a stronger incentive to lobby against the parents' recommendations than the parents will have to lobby in favor of them.

It is clear, then, that public school employees are better able to lobby for spending increases and policy decisions they support than are parents. When we look at the Chicago Public Schools today, we see the results of over one hundred years of this uneven competition between school employees and community representatives. The size and cost of the system's bureaucracy are the most visible results.

Accountability and Choice

Despite the centralization of the Chicago Public School system and the large bureaucracy, it is still possible that the schools could be held accountable to the public. This would occur if parents could choose the school their children would attend.

If a mechanism existed whereby parents could choose their child's school, individual schools that were failing to provide a safe and positive learning environment could lose students to those that did. Soon a bottom line would emerge for these schools, and they would have to begin listening to parents' suggestions in order to get back their enrollment. If enough parents thought the Chicago Public Schools were too centralized or wasteful, they could enroll their children in competing private schools or suburban public school systems. This would create a competitive pressure on the Chicago Public Schools to reduce its bureaucracy, open its doors to concerned parents and community members, and perhaps even experiment with smaller schools or different enrollment policies. The result would be a school system that is more accountable to its clients.

Unfortunately, the Chicago Public Schools make choice very costly for parents today. A parent who has tried without success to improve a public school's policies may not elect to enroll a child in a different public school: enrollment (except for the exclusive magnet schools) is determined by where the child lives. Parents may tolerate the problem and place their children at risk, or withdraw the children from the public school system and enroll them in a different public school system or a private school. But these options are very expensive: to enroll in a suburban public school the family must move to a new home (or, as some low-income families do, engage in an illegal plan to misrepresent where the child actually lives). To enroll a child in a private school, a parent must both pay tuition *and* continue to pay taxes to the public schools.

The parents of over 126,000 children enrolled in nonpublic schools in Chicago *have* made the choice to leave the public schools. After the 1987 Chicago school strike the parents of an additional 11,500 children chose not to return their children to the public schools. However, parents do this at great personal sacrifice. Because the cost of exercising this option is so high, the staff of poor public schools know they are effectively protected from competition, either from better public schools or from private schools. Consequently, they are protected from the consequences of parental and community dissatisfaction.

By geographic assignment of students, the Chicago Public Schools restrict the ability of parents to select the public school of their choice. By not giving tax relief to parents who pay tuition at private schools, the current school system penalizes parents who choose to remove their children from the public school system. An administrator's job is not at risk if parents are not free to withdraw their children from the offending school. Knowing that parents are forced to enroll their children at the local public school, administrators are likely to be much less responsive to parents' criticism and suggestions.

A crucial difference between the Chicago Public Schools and private schools is that the public schools do not run the risk of being defunded or abandoned by dissatisfied parents, whereas private schools do.

Most students -- particularly those with parents who lack the sophistication to work the system -- have no choice of which public school they will attend; they are assigned to the school in their district. Again, if parents choose to enroll their child in a private school, they must still pay taxes to support the public school they do not wish to use. As a result, the income of the public school does not change when parents become dissatisfied.

Conclusion

In this chapter we focused our attention on three factors in the decline of the Chicago Public Schools: barriers to parental participation, the growth of a large bureaucracy, and the absence of accountability. These factors were the outcome of specific causes: centralized administration; the absence of a bottom line and the presence of perverse incentive structures in the schools; the tendency for public employees to out-organize parents and community members; and the practice of geographic assignment of students to schools.

A decision made over one hundred years ago to impose a common curriculum on all school-age children in America has resulted in a centralized administration and unaccountable bureaucracy in the city of Chicago. The price has been steep: parents locked out of important decision-making processes, and administrators free from the discipline of the bottom line. The solution that is beginning to emerge calls for decentralization, competition, and choice.

Notes

1. See U.S. Department of Education, *What Works* (1986), p. 19, for citations. See also James S. Coleman and Thomas Hoffer, *Public and Private High Schools: The Impact of Communities* (New York: Basic Books, 1987).

2. For a review of the literature, see Herbert J. Walberg, "Families as Partners in Educational Productivity," *Phi Delta Kappan* 84, No. 6 (1984), pp. 397-400.

3. Herbert J. Walberg and G. Alfred Hess, Jr., *Chicagoans View Their Public Schools* (Chicago Panel On Public School Finances, June 1985). This survey found that large majorities of parents believe principals should have more authority to run their schools, including the hiring and firing of teachers and the selection of subjects taught.

4. Laura Washington, "Evaluation System Fails, Gives Problem Teachers a Pass," *Chicago Reporter*, July 1982.

5. "Parents flunk budgets for public schools," *Chicago Tribune*, March 9, 1988.

6. "Disillusioned parents balk at school budget vote," *Chicago Tribune*, March 10, 1988.

7. In this section the authors are summarizing a variety of theories that together come under the label "public choice." Good descriptions of this emerging scholarship can be found in Gordon Tullock, *Private Wants, Public Means* (Latham, MD: University Press of America, Inc., 1987); Dennis C. Mueller, *Public Choice* (New York: Cambridge University Press, 1979 (1987)); and William A. Niskanen, Jr., *Bureaucracy and Representative Government* (Chicago: Aldine-Atherton, 1971).

8. Myrom Lieberman, "Market Solutions to the Education Crisis," *Cato Policy Analysis #75*, July 1, 1986, p. 1.

6

POVERTY, ETHNICITY, AND OTHER BARRIERS TO EXCELLENCE

[I]t is a sad fact that too many schools in disadvantaged communities are failing to provide the majority of their students with the skills they will need to lead successful lives. Therefore, the restructuring of schools must be made a priority in communities whose children suffer serious problems of poverty and discrimination.

Committee for
Economic Development
Children in Need

Chicago's schools face many special challenges caused by poverty, ethnicity, crime, and other factors. These factors do not excuse the Chicago Public Schools of every shortcoming or inadequacy they may have, but they do form an important background and context that must be recognized and evaluated before judgments may be made. The fate of disadvantaged children in inner-city public schools makes the path to excellence in education very complicated, since some changes made in the name of reform would reduce our commitment to providing equal educational opportunity to all children. In this chapter, we ask whether the problems of inner-city living make excellence unobtainable in large cities such as Chicago, and what accommodations and special efforts can be made by the schools in response to them.

"Excellence" and the Disadvantaged Child

"Excellence" in education has become a catch-word, with much of the debate skirting the difficult task of actually defining it. It is generally agreed that excellence has something to do with restoring standards and getting tougher about what is taught and how things are taught. Common sense ideas like recruiting better-prepared teachers and making students write more have become fashionable. Even insisting that students do homework again is part of this reform agenda.

But we must ask whether *all* children can achieve excellence. What happens to those students, seemingly present in large numbers in urban schools, who simply cannot keep up with rising standards and the return to academic discipline? Will the pursuit of excellence be an excuse for leaving behind those children whose home life, culture, or bodies make it difficult to conform to the latest program's formula and procedures?

The National Coalition of Advocates for Students has taken the lead in addressing the problems of children at risk. Their report, *Barriers to Excellence: Our Children at Risk*, identified needed school changes in terms of the problems of students whose "learning is hampered by schools who do not

76

serve them adequately; by expectations on the part of educators that they will or cannot succeed; by denial to special access programs; by fiscal policies that limit educational services; and by inattention to the difficulties young people face in moving from school to work."[1] They identified these at-risk children as young people of all races who were poor, immigrants who faced discrimination, girls and young women who were denied educational opportunities because of their sex, and children with special needs who were not served or were incorrectly categorized because of their learning difficulties.

These educators saw the excellence movement as embracing "quick-fix solutions that will not readily improve the quality of education."[2] Primarily working in inner-city communities, they witnessed firsthand the growing decay of urban schools, the increasing pathology of ghetto life, and the economic and psychological despair that comes with being unable to find or hold a job. These educators took upon themselves the task of forcing America to face the facts about its cities and the schools that are in them.

Ethnicity

Approximately 60 percent of the students in the Chicago Public Schools are black, 23 percent are Hispanic, and 14 percent are white. The number of white students has fallen dramatically since 1970, from two hundred thousand enrolled in that year to fewer than sixty thousand in 1985-86. The fall in white enrollment has been particularly apparent in the high schools, where it fell 37 percent during the first five years of this decade.[3]

Black enrollment, as a percentage of total enrollment in the public school system, peaked at 61 percent in 1980 and has since fallen by a percentage point. Surging Hispanic enrollment accounts for the change, rising from 9.7 percent of total enrollment in

1970 to 23 percent in 1985-86. Blacks and Hispanics, then, together account for over 80 percent of the Chicago Public Schools' enrollment.

Public schools in Chicago seem unable to accommodate the growing presence of minority students in the classroom. Approximately 50 percent of Hispanic and black students in the Class of 1982 dropped out before graduating.[4] The Hispanic drop-out rate in Chicago's *inner-city* public schools was a shocking 70 percent, second only to New York's 80 percent.[5]

Unless public schools begin to address the special needs of black and Hispanic students, these problems will grow larger. Today the majority of students in the largest twenty-five city school systems are cultural minorities, while in 1950 a mere 10 percent of the student population in the large districts was minority. By 1990, one of every three students in the public schools will be a minority. In Chicago, the already small number of white students may further diminish as the number of Hispanic, black, and Asian students continues to rise.

As former U.S. Commissioner of Education Dr. Ernest L. Boyer warned, the educational system will be faced with "a group of children who will be poorer, more ethnically and linguistically diverse, and have more handicaps that surely will affect their schooling."[6] We are, he says, developing a kind of educational Third World within our inner cities.

Poverty

Economic and social problems also create trouble for the schools. The number of poor households headed by a black or Hispanic female is increasing dramatically, with 90 percent of the increase in children born into poverty coming from these households. Although two-thirds of all the nation's poor children are white, the percentage of black children living with one parent who is poor is

78

much higher, and of those children who remain in poverty for more than four years, blacks represent a heavy majority.[7]

In 1974, for the first time, children became the poorest segment of American society. In the years since, the extent of their poverty has become more widespread. By 1984, nearly one-quarter of all children under age seventeen lived in poverty. Among blacks, one of every two lived in poverty, among Hispanics two of every five.

Poverty has many negative effects on schools. Children arrive at schools hungry or, even worse, malnourished. Worthy role models at home or in the child's local community are scarce, so attempts by the school to guide a child's development are continually frustrated. Poverty drives a wedge between parents and the schools by causing parents to move frequently or temporarily transfer custody of their children to better-off relatives or family friends. It is not unusual for teachers at inner-city public schools to have up-to-date addresses for only a third or fewer of the children they teach. Frequent parent-teacher discussions obviously are made difficult.

Immigration

Another important factor influencing education in major cities is immigration, both legal and illegal. In 1984, approximately 544,000 people immigrated legally to America, roughly the annual average during the 1920s. Add to this number the three hundred thousand to five hundred thousand people who entered the nation illegally, and 1984 immigration totals exceed any past year's total.[8] Most of these new arrivals came to our cities and placed additional pressures on our urban schools.

While this is not the first time cities have been the magnet for immigrants, racial minorities, or the poor, the magnitude of the projected numbers today is cause for concern. In previous eras, escape routes were available and visible -- unskilled labor was in demand by factories and dockyards, for example, and the public schools offered an education that had demonstrable value in the job market. Today these options are limited. There are fewer and fewer opportunities for factory work, and the urban schools seem not to work at all.

In addition to ethnicity-based cultural and linguistic challenges, immigrants face problems as newcomers to a large urban environment. Immigrant children often lack even the familiarity with the larger culture that domestic ethnic groups gain through television and radio. The children face alienation at home, in a strange new community, and in the schools. Uncertainty over the legal status of many of today's immigrants can make immigrant parents reluctant to communicate with teachers, school administrators, and other agents of the larger culture.

A Handicap or an Insurmountable Barrier?

Although ethnicity, poverty, and immigration are documented and persistent problems facing public schools in many large cities, it is not necessary to conclude that these problems are insurmountable. What do we know of the overall achievement of children who face these problems, and what can this information tell us about the prospects for excellence in the inner city?

Extensive research has failed to find a close correlation between the wealth and occupation of a student's family and how well children learn in school. K.R. White in 1976 collected some 636 correlations of socioeconomic indices with ability and academic achievement from 101 studies. His synthesis found that socioeconomic status counts on average only for about 6 percent of the variance in learning.[9] Although on average children from families with higher socioeconomic measures outperform children from families with lower measures, many children from the less well-off families outperform their middle-class peers. Thus, contrary to the great importance given to parental socioeconomic status by some sociologists, its association with learning is surprisingly weak.

The presence of examples of high achievement by poor black and Hispanic youths in some schools, both public and private, also lends support to the idea that poverty and ethnicity do not always stand in the way of excellence. For example, over 80 percent of the students enrolled in Chicago's Catholic schools are minorities, yet over half go on to college. (The record of the Catholic schools will be discussed in more detail in Chapter Seven.) Just two of the many unaffiliated schools in Chicago that have become well known for their accomplishments with low-income students are Marva Collins' Westside Preparatory School and Mary Mays' Accounters Preparatory Academy.

Westside Preparatory School

The Westside Preparatory School is probably Chicago's most famous school serving minority students from low-income families.[10] The school was founded by educator Marva Collins in 1975, shortly after she resigned as a public school teacher. Prior to starting the school, she had taught in a public school for thirteen years during the 1960s and 1970s. Westside Prep was brought to the nation's attention in 1977 when it was profiled by *Time* magazine, and its founder has been the subject of extensive press coverage ever since.

Starting in a single room and later occupying the second floor of Collins' Garfield Park two-flat, the school relocated in 1981 to its current building at 4146 West Chicago Avenue. The school has a 1987-88 enrollment of 225 children, with tuition

81

ranging from entirely grant supported to $260 per month. The student population is predominantly black but racially mixed.

Attempts to measure the success of Westside Prep have been controversial. Collins is able to document substantial improvements in standardized test scores for most students, and sometimes dramatic improvements in as little as a few months. She recruits students who are believed to have behavioral problems and learning disabilities, and uses her unique brand of "tough love" to alter their conduct and direct their attention to learning. A sometimes harsh critic of the public schools, she has herself been the target of harsh criticism from public school teachers and administrators.

Looking past the controversy, there is general agreement that Marva Collins' approach to education has, for many disadvantaged children, meant the difference between failure and genuine learning. Further evidence of her success includes the dramatic growth of her school and the successful admission of many of her graduates to prestigious private schools and academies.

Why has Westside Prep been so successful? Excerpts from *Marva Collins' Way* may be the best way to capture the philosophy and structure of this school. So here is Marva Collins on...

...creating a sense of camaraderie and mission:

> Learning was to be a group effort. Everyone in the school was part of the team, and like any team, the school would only work if everyone pulled together. . . . Our class had to be a support group, urging one another along and delighting in each other's small accomplishments, much the way a group of Weight Watchers rallies around a new dieter or an Alcoholics Anonymous meeting takes a new member under wing.[11]

...homework:

I gave homework every day, though never in massive doses. A child should not have to do thirty math problems overnight. Five or ten problems are enough to see if a child knows what he is doing. I didn't give homework as busy work, but to reinforce a lesson. And I never gave homework until I was certain that the child could do it successfully.[12]

...classroom discipline:

Everyone knew there would be no gum chewing, nail biting, unbuttoned shirts, loose shirt tails, jazzy walks, jive talk, or finger snapping.[13]

...and on curriculum:

The great books were their greatest teacher. While there are critics who claim the classics are too difficult for younger students to read, . . . I have found that great literature not only teaches students to read but makes them thirsty for more and more knowledge. These books *are* over the head of the student reader; that is the purpose of reading them. We read to stretch the mind, to seek, to strive, to wonder, and then reread.[14]

Not all good schools share Westside Prep's emphasis on discipline or the "great books," but there are school policies described here that most parents will recognize and support. Strong instructional leadership, an emphasis on basic skills, and high teacher expectations for student achievement are essential components of the Westside Prep success story. That these traits can work in one of Chicago's poorest neighborhoods is reassuring news for everyone concerned with education for disadvantaged children.

Accounters Preparatory Academy

Another inner-city success story, this one on the city's South Side, is Accounters Preparatory Academy, located at 7949 South Ashland.[15] Founded in 1974 by Mary M. Mays as an outgrowth of weekend and summer tutoring programs begun seven years earlier, the school enrolls seventy students in grades kindergarten through eighth. Perhaps what is most distinctive about this school is the degree of parental involvement. According to Mays:

> Parents come in once a month. We expect every parent to participate, *every parent*. Parents have to become involved with children. It's only two hours. We tell them that's less than one 24-hour day a year.[16]

Tuition at Accounters Prep is $950 per year for kindergarten through third grade, and $1,250 per year for fourth through eighth grades. Combinations of work and grants are used to help those who cannot otherwise afford the tuition. Curriculum focuses on the basics and learning through repetition. Textbooks are carefully selected for the standards they set. According to Accounters' principal, Reggee McClinton:

I teach them not to be satisfied. If they're in third grade, they read third-grade books. Nothing is watered down. Our teachers use the 1979 edition of the reader because the new ones require fewer skills. No one is allowed to have excuses, period. When you teach children this they expect it of themselves.[17]

Most students at Accounters Prep perform at one to two years above their grade levels, and as of October 1986 every child who had ever graduated from the school was either in college or employed. Classes at the school are remarkable for their orderliness and air of quiet study. This record of accomplishment is all the more remarkable considering the background of the children: 60 percent are from single-parent homes, all are black, and most live in the low-income neighborhood of the school.

Why does Accounters Preparatory Academy work? Author Lillian Thomas, who profiled the school in a Chicago *Reader* article in 1986, identified seven factors at work: strong leadership, high expectations, discipline, a curriculum with cultural content, a sense of camaraderie or companionship, mandatory parental involvement, and the kind of efficiency and prioritizing that comes with severe underfunding.

That this school, like Westside Preparatory, is producing well-educated youths adds further support for the proposition that all children can learn if given the proper school environment.

Conclusion

Can disadvantaged children learn as fast or as well as the children of upper-income families? To Marva Collins and Mary Mays, the answer is clear.

As Collins says:

> To me it seems perfectly plain that
> inner-city children should be taught
> the same way other children are
> taught, because all children want the
> same things out of life. A ghetto
> child learns the same way as any
> other child and is equally capable of
> reading Dante, Homer, Pascal, or
> Chaucer.[18]

We can reach two conclusions. First, it is
beyond debate that the Chicago Public Schools face
difficulties caused by the city's urban environment.
Educating children who are hungry, or who come
from broken homes or very different ethnic cultures,
must be more difficult than teaching children who
have been assimilated to the culture of the larger,
middle-class society. But our second conclusion must
be that these difficulties are overcome by some
schools in Chicago. These schools exhibit traits--
such as high expectations, orderly classrooms, and a
sense of camaraderie -- that are linked to their
success and conspicuously absent from many public
schools. We conclude, quite simply, that poverty and
ethnicity present problems that can be overcome.

Notes

1. National Coalition of Advocates for Students, *Barriers to Excellence: Our Children at Risk* (Boston, January 1985).
2. Designs for Change, *Our Children at Risk: The Crisis in Public Education* (Chicago, 1984), p. 5.
3. Chicago Panel on Public School Policy and Finance, *Who Benefits from Desegregation?* (Chicago, December 1987), pp. 7, 19.
4. Floyd Morgan Hammack, "Large School Systems' Dropout Reports: An Analysis of Definitions, Procedures, and Findings," Spring 1986, p. 330.
5. National Commission on Secondary Education for Hispanics, *Make Something Happen*, 1984, p. 23.
6. Ernest L. Boyer, "Improve Urban Schools or Face Educational Third World, Boyer Warns," *State Education Leader*, Education Commission of the States, Vol. 5, No. 4, December 1986.
7. Michael D. Usdan, "New Trends in Urban Demography," *Education and Urban Society*, Vol. 16, No. 4, August 1984.
8. "Here They Come, Ready or Not," *Education Week*, May 14, 1986, p. 16.
9. K.R. White, "The Relation Between Socioeconomic Status and Academic Achievement," *Psychological Bulletin*, 91 (3), pp. 461-481.
10. Most of the information for this chapter is taken from Marva Collins and Civia Tamarkin, *Marva Collins' Way* (Los Angeles: Jeremy P. Tarcher, Inc., 1982), and a telephone interview with Sharon Miner, Mrs. Collins' secretary, on March 16, 1988.
11. Collins and Tamarkin, *Marva Collins' Way*, p. 115.
12. Ibid., pp. 132-33.
13. Ibid., p. 140.
14. Ibid., p. 178.

15. This profile is based on conversations with Mary Mays and Reggee McClinton; an article by Lillian Thomas titled "Small Successes," *Reader* (Chicago), October 3, 1986; and Joan Davis Ratteray, "Access to Quality: Private Schools in Chicago's Inner City" (Chicago: The Heartland Institute, June 27, 1986).

16. Thomas.

17. Ibid., p. 34

18. Collins and Tamarkin, *Marva Collins' Way*, p. 185.

7

WHY SOME SCHOOLS WORK

The most important characteristics of effective schools are strong instructional leadership, a safe and orderly climate, school-wide emphasis on basic skills, high teacher expectations for student achievement, and continuous assessment of pupil progress.

U.S. Dept. of Education
What Works

There is a large and growing body of empirical research concerning the effectiveness of different educational techniques. In addition, there are schools that we can visit where teachers and administrators listen to taxpayers, respect the input of parents, and educate children well. These schools are both public and private, and they are diverse in terms of race, religion, and ethnicity.[1] What lessons can we learn from this literature and these schools that will help us redesign the Chicago Public Schools?

The Nine Factors of Learning

In recent years several scientific breakthroughs have occurred in the analysis of large-scale educational surveys and in the synthesis of thousands of educational research results. A synthesis of some 2,575 educational studies suggests that nine factors increase learning. Potent, consistent, and widely generalizable, these nine factors fall into three groups: student aptitude, instruction, and psychological environment.[2]

While many aspects of these factors--especially the amount and quality of instruction--can be altered by educators, many are beyond their control. For example, a school's curriculum, particularly in terms of length of time devoted to various subjects and activities, is partly determined by economic, political, and social forces. Ability and motivation, moreover, are influenced by parents, by prior learning, and by students themselves. Thus educators are unlikely to raise achievement substantially by their own efforts alone.

The powerful influences of out-of-school factors, especially the so-called "curriculum of the home," must be recognized by advocates of school reform. Twelve years of elementary and secondary school add up to only about 13 percent of the waking, potentially educative time during the first eighteen years of life. If more of the student's time spent outside school were spent in academically stimulating conditions in the home and with peer groups, then the student's total learning time might be raised beyond the time spent in school. For instance, the average high school student spends twenty-eight hours a week viewing television but only four or five hours on homework.[3] Certainly academic performance could be improved by shifting time from television viewing to performing homework.

The factors of educational productivity

Student Aptitude

1. **Ability,** or preferably prior achievement, as measured by the usual achievement tests.

2. **Development** as indexed by chronological age or stage of maturation.

3. **Motivation** or self-concept as indicated by personality tests or by the student's willingness to persevere intensively on learning tasks.

Instruction

4. The **amount** of time a student engages in learning.

5. The **quality** of the instructional experience, including psychological and curricular aspects.

Psychological Environment

6. The "**curriculum of the home.**"

7. The **morale** of the classroom social group.

8. The **peer group** outside school.

9. Amount of leisure-time **television** viewing.

At least one public school in Chicago, Grant School on the city's West Side, has implemented a successful program to improve the curriculum of the home. Committees composed of staff and parents set goals and met periodically during the summer and school year. Part of the program involved performance contracts signed by the principal, teachers, parents, and students. Teachers pledged to provide specific services to a child; parents pledged to provide a quiet and well-lit place for study each day; students pledged to study for certain lengths of time and strive to attain certain performance goals. The contract bound parents, teachers, and students more closely together, and moved the learning process from the school into the home.[4]

A number of specific instructional methods have been found to have powerful and consistent influences on learning. Quantitative syntheses of studies show that some methods are far more effective than others that are commonly used in schools today, and yet they are not necessarily more costly.[5] Some of the more effective methods are:

mastery learning, including Skinnerian reinforcement and acknowledgement of correct performance. Other features of mastery learning -- appropriate instructional cues, continuous engagement of students in lessons, and corrective feedback in cases of student errors -- also have significant effects.[6]

acceleration programs, which provide college-level lessons and other advanced activities to elementary and high school students with outstanding scores on difficult selection tests. Students in these programs gain much more than comparable control groups.

reading training, or programs that coach learners in adjusting reading speed and techniques to purposes such as skimming, comprehension, and finding answers to questions. The unusual learning criterion in assessing these programs is reader adaptability to purpose and material.

92

Other instructional programs and methods that have significant and consistent effects include *cooperative team learning*, in which some autonomy over the means and pace of learning is delegated to students who form small groups to help each other, and *personalized and adaptive instruction* such as tutoring and diagnostic-prescriptive methods. Probably more teachers would employ such training techniques if they knew of their effectiveness and if they were trained to do so.

Although these methods have been well demonstrated in classroom research, they are not widespread in practice. As is the case with other scientific discoveries, it may take considerable time for superior techniques to become popular in practice, especially when they require extra preparation and uncompensated entrepreneurial work on the part of practitioners. An important question to ask of school reform proposals, therefore, is whether they increase the ability of schools to adopt these proven instructional methods, and reward those teachers and principals who invest in mastering them.

Research on Effective Schools

What kinds of schools are most likely to influence positively the nine factors that increase learning? A review of the massive literature on effective schools has produced a commonly repeated "formula" for success. It has been summarized as follows in a U.S. Department of Education publication titled *What Works*:

> The most important characteristics of effective schools are strong instructional leadership, a safe and orderly climate, school-wide emphasis on basic skills, high teacher expectations for student achievement, and continuous assessment of pupil progress.[7]

93

These characteristics are remarkably similar to those of Accounters Preparatory Academy and Westside Prep, the two successful schools profiled in the last chapter. Unfortunately, too few of the Chicago Public Schools fit this description.

One characteristic, "strong instructional leadership," concerns the role of the principal in a school. In the Chicago Public Schools, principals lack many of the powers needed to exercise leadership in instruction, making it difficult for any school in the system to fulfill the formula. In Chapter One we discussed the lack of safety in the Chicago Public Schools, and in Chapter Five we saw how barriers to parental involvement and the absence of accountability make it unlikely that teachers or principals will be motivated and responsive to students' needs. The structure of the Chicago Public Schools, then, prevents individual schools from excelling.

An environment that fosters selection of effective teaching methods and the other characteristics of effective schools does not just happen. Only through deliberate organization or structure is such a result possible. Reporting on his research for the Brookings Institution, John E. Chubb writes:

> Those organizational qualities that we consider to be essential ingredients of an effective school -- such things as academically focused objectives, pedagogically strong principals, relatively autonomous teachers, and collegial staff relations -- do not flourish without the willingness of superintendents, school boards, or other outside authorities to delegate meaningful control over school policy, personnel, and practice to the school itself. Efforts to improve the performance of schools without changing the way they are organized or the controls they respond to will therefore probably meet with no more than modest success; they are even more likely to be undone.[8]

Thus, the way schools are organized and how school systems are structured are of crucial importance. While the right kind of organization can encourage the development of those ingredients necessary to an effective school, the wrong kind of organization can discourage or prevent them from developing.

What Does Not Work?

In addition to noting what works in schooling, it is important that we also be aware of what does not work. Just as statistical synthesis of empirical research has revealed the components of an effective school, so too has it exposed "reforms" that produce no positive results.

Higher teacher salaries and smaller class sizes (except class sizes of less than ten) have been found repeatedly to have no significant positive effect on learning.[9] Similarly, total spending per pupil is unrelated to educational results, as are administrators' salaries and teacher experience.[10] In reviewing studies of school district expenditure equalization, two independent researchers concluded that increased expenditures go mainly into administrative and auxiliary activities that have little or no effect on educational outcomes.[11]

The most comprehensive synthesis of the possible effects of total expenditures and specific inputs on achievement also shows no consistent association between expenditures and learning. From a quantitative synthesis of 130 econometric studies, E.A. Hanushek concluded:

> The available evidence suggests that there is no relationship between expenditures and achievement of students, and that such traditional remedies as reducing class sizes or hiring better trained teachers are unlikely to improve matters.[12]

A 1987 study of school districts in New Jersey found that "per-student financial expenditures on education are insignificantly or inconsistently associated with achievement test scores. Low-spending districts on average achieve as well as high-spending districts of the same socioeconomic status."[13] Other studies could also be cited.

The unavoidable conclusion of this body of research is that spending more money on ineffective schools does not produce better results. Higher pay for teachers, smaller class sizes, and more spending on support services have all been put forward as necessary "reforms" in Chicago and other cities around the country. But careful and repeated research reveals that such proposals are bound to disappoint their supporters.

A Case Study: Catholic Schools in Chicago

A discussion of "what works" cannot be complete without mention of Chicago's Catholic schools.[14] Very simply, the Catholic schools work. Spokespersons for the schools say they do not wish to compete with the public schools. They believe their schools have an important role to play in providing a quality, values-oriented education to families in Chicago's inner city. But whether or not they directly compete with the public school system for students, the successes of Catholic schools clearly present a challenge to the city's public schools.

Existing side-by-side with Chicago's public schools are the 124 inner-city elementary schools and sixteen inner-city high schools of the Catholic Archdiocese of Chicago. More than 48,000 students are enrolled in these schools. (The Archdiocese of Chicago operates a total of 408 schools enrolling over 161,000 students throughout Cook and Lake counties.) In the words of a Catholic priest involved in the schools, "we have two public school systems in Chicago, one financed with taxes and the other with private funds."[15]

A comparison of the students attending the two systems reveals remarkable similarities: over 80 percent of the student enrollment of both school systems is minority. Both school systems draw students from the surrounding low-income neighborhoods, and except for tuition charged by the Catholic schools both have what amounts to open enrollment policies. Many of the Catholic schools have scholarship funds for families unable to pay the modest tuition, which averages $700 for elementary schools and $1,700 for high schools.[16] Some Catholic schools allow students to perform janitorial tasks in exchange for free or reduced tuition.[17] Forty percent of the students in Chicago Catholic schools are non-Catholic.

It is popularly imagined that Catholic schools are able to outperform public schools only because they recruit students from white and upper-income families. In fact, this is not the case. James Coleman reports that "the income distribution of families of students who attend schools in the private sector is not greatly different from that in the public sector."[18] Alfredo Lanier, writing for *Chicago* magazine, found that this is particularly true of inner-city schools in Chicago:

> In reality, most inner-city parochial schools have no stringent admission standards. Notes the principal of a parochial school whose students come mostly from a public housing project: "In this neighborhood it's hard to take the cream of the crop, because there isn't much cream to be found."[19]

Though they teach children from the same socioeconomic backgrounds, Catholic schools and public schools in Chicago produce dramatically different results. Catholic schools in Chicago report a dropout rate of less than 1 percent, compared to 50

97

percent for the public schools. Over seventy percent of Chicago Catholic school graduates go on to college or other specialized training.[20] Because the Archdiocese discontinued uniform testing for its schools some years ago, it is not possible to say with certainty how the school systems compare with regard to standardized tests. However, most observers conclude that their test scores would conform with the findings reported in Chapter Two. That is, children from the same socioeconomic backgrounds enrolled in Catholic high schools advance up to two grade levels for every one level of advancement by students enrolled in neighborhood public schools.

Most anecdotal descriptions of Catholic schools in Chicago describe policies and practices that correspond closely to the U.S. Department of Education's prescription for an effective school.[21] Violence against pupils or teachers is almost unheard of; orderly classrooms and strictly enforced dress codes are the rule; principals wield substantial authority over curricula and personnel; parental involvement is actively encouraged and in some schools required. A sense of pride in the students and the school pervades many of the schools.

This evaluation of Catholic schools as "schools that work" is supported by teachers who work in public and Catholic high schools. A 1984 survey asked teachers to judge their "school climate" in such areas as teacher morale, principal leadership, staff cooperation, and student behavior. Teachers in Catholic schools consistently ranked the climates of their schools better than did their public school counterparts.[22]

How do they do it? How do Catholic schools in Chicago produce better results, at lower cost, for students drawn from the same backgrounds as children in the city's failing public schools? The answer to this question is much disputed in educational research and in public discourse.

Some observers contend that it is the superior motivation of parents with children attending Catholic schools, not the Catholic schools themselves, that

School Climate in Public and Catholic High Schools, as Judged by Teachers, 1984

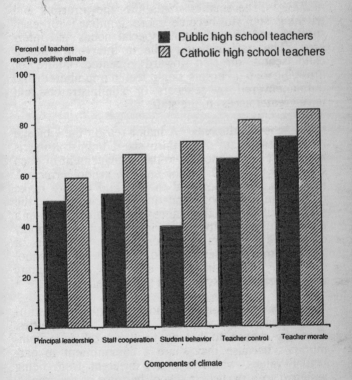

Percent of teachers
reporting positive climate

■ Public high school teachers
▨ Catholic high school teachers

Components of climate

SOURCE: High School and Beyond Administrator and Teacher Survey,
Center for Education Statistics analysis.

is responsible for the observed differences in school outputs. But it is more likely that Catholic schools *produce* motivated parents by giving parents greater opportunities to participate in the operation of the schools.[23] Three features of Catholic schools, in particular, seem to encourage parental involvement:

Smaller schools. The average Catholic school in Chicago enrolls approximately four hundred students, compared to the average enrollment in public schools of 723.[24] The smaller size allows the principal and teaching staff to become more familiar with each student, and to understand special needs and interests. The staff is better able to intervene when a child seems directed toward repeated failure or dropping out. Parents don't feel outnumbered and outmaneuvered by teachers or administrators and have greater access to the staff.

Local school autonomy. A major reason the Chicago Archdiocese has only thirty-six administrators is because it leaves the day-to-day management of each school to the parish pastor and the school principal. Principals are empowered to hire and fire, to make curriculum decisions, and to take charge of the school building's maintenance and repair. Being in a position of authority, the principal can and usually does give teachers and community volunteers a greater role in setting and implementing school policies. This, in turn, encourages community involvement in the school and teacher self-esteem.

Voluntary enrollment. Catholic schools are institutions created by voluntary religious communities. Families choose to belong to these religious communities because they share a commitment to particular values, which is much different from being assigned to a particular school because of geography. Catholic children attend Catholic schools as a way to participate in their family's religious community, and they become part of their parents' social network in the process.[25] Non-Catholic students are drawn into

100

this "value community" too, since inner-city Catholic schools stress ecumenical themes and are often important centers of social activities.

Of these three factors -- size, autonomy, and voluntary enrollment -- the last is perhaps the most important. Parents who enroll their children in schools of choice have a sense of ownership and responsibility toward that school. Parents of children enrolled in Catholic schools have more opportunities and more reasons to interact with one another and with the staff and leadership of the local school than do the parents of children in a public school. This interaction *empowers* them by helping them to share information, develop relationships with teachers and principals, and organize their own efforts to assist and supervise the schools. So empowered, they can more effectively intervene in their children's education through discipline, encouragement, or other forms of special attention.[26]

Families with children in public schools, because they are assigned to schools based on geography, also are likely to have certain interests in common. But during the years since the public schools first were formed, various social and economic changes (such as the separation of home and work and improved transportation) have reduced the importance of spatial proximity in building a sense of community, and increased the role of shared interests and values.[27] This trend has strengthened private schools -- built on foundations of values and interests -- at the same time it has hurt public schools, whose enrollments are usually determined by geographic assignment.

Catholic schools in Chicago have escaped the causes of decline that have affected the Chicago Public Schools. Since parents are free to withdraw their children from the schools if they become dissatisfied, the schools are naturally more *accountable* to parents. Since they stand to lose income if parents withdraw their children, the Catholic schools have not been allowed to lose sight of their bottom line. Since the schools are smaller and the parents better organized, the imbalance between organized school employees and unorganized parents is less pronounced and damaging. Oppourtunities for parental participation and scrutiny of school policies have not been denied.

There are many other factors that distinguish the Chicago Catholic school system from the Chicago Public Schools, but these factors all seem to lead back to the basic issues of accountability, local school autonomy, and voluntary enrollment. For example, different policies regarding merit pay for teachers, teacher salaries, and teacher participation in school management all can be traced to autonomy and empowered principals. Violence, dropout rates, drug abuse, and teenage pregnancy are symptoms of a school that is too big for adequate supervision of troubled students and a community that lacks effective methods of intervention.

Conclusion

Learning is a complex social activity that relies on a variety of factors, not all of which are under the control of educators. However, effective schools have been able to motivate parents, teachers, administrators, and students to influence positively these factors and produce superior results. Avenues for public participation in school management are essential for developing the accountability and sense of community membership that characterize these schools.

One road that does *not* lead to effective schools is increased spending on existing school structures. Over and over again, researchers have found that higher levels of spending do not lead to better educational results. Teachers' salaries and class size have also been found to be unrelated to the quality of schooling. Real reform requires something other than more funding: it requires structural change.

We can see in the Catholic schools a promise that effective schools are possible in Chicago's inner city. Moreover, the Catholic schools prove that good schools need not be selective or restricted only to social or economic elites, but can be open to all Chicagoans. We have also seen that the structure of these effective schools is quite different from that of the Chicago Public Schools, and that many of the differences in outcome can be attributed to this structure.

1. See Joan Davis Ratteray, "Access to Quality: Private Schools in Chicago's Inner City" (Chicago: The Heartland Institute, June 27, 1986); Daniel L. Schultz, "Lessons from America's Best Run Schools," *The Washington Monthly*, November 1983; and Thomas Sowell, "Patterns of Black Excellence," *The Public Interest*, No. 43, Spring 1976, pp. 26-58.

2. Herbert Walberg and his colleagues have published roughly two dozen empirical studies in research journals of the American Educational Research Association and the American Psychological Association. Only after extensive observation and some modifications to the theory did these researchers present the implications of their work in professional and policy journals such as *Daedalus*, *Educational Leadership*, and *Phi Delta Kappan*. Like other explicit scientific theories, however, the theory of educational productivity should be considered open to disproof in part or whole by empirical contradiction.

3. Herbert J. Walberg and T. Shanahan, "High School Effects on Individual Students," *Educational Researcher* 12, No. 7 (1983), pp. 4-9.

4. Herbert J. Walberg, "Families as Partners in Educational Productivity," *Phi Delta Kappan*, Vol. 84, No. 6 (1984), pp. 397-400.

5. Herbert J. Walberg and W.J. Fowler, "Expenditure and Size Efficiencies of Public School Districts," *Educational Researcher* 16, No. 7 (1987), pp. 5-15.

6. Mastery learning was begun as a supplemental program in the Chicago Public Schools in the early 1970s and became the system's primary reading and math program in the early 1980s. The program was so controversial that Manford Byrd, Jr.'s first official act as superintendent in

1985 was to appoint committees to reexamine the program. The program's highly structured approach to learning has led some educators to say it stifles creativity and is less personal than traditional teaching methods. The lesson, if there is one, may be that a teaching method that is good in theory may be disappointing in practice if it is imposed in the typical top-down manner that prevails today in school districts across the nation and in Chicago. See "Byrd is Already Talking Reform," *Chicago Tribune*, March 26, 1985.

7. U.S. Dept. of Education, *What Works* (1986), p. 44. Herbert J. Walberg was a key contributor to this publication. See also Bruce Fuller, "Defining School Quality," in *The Contribution of the Social Sciences to Educational Policy and Practice: 1965-1985*, edited by Jane Hannaway and Marlaine E. Lockheed (Berkeley: McCutchan Publishing Corporation, 1986), p. 34.

8. John E. Chubb, "Why the Current Wave of School Reform Will Fail," *The Public Interest*, No. 90, Winter 1988, p. 29.

9. R.G. Bridge, C.M. Judd, and P.R. Moock, *The Determinants of Educational Outcomes: The Impact of Families, Peers, Teachers, and Schools* (Cambridge, MA: Ballinger Publishing Co., 1979). Also G.V. Glass, L. Cahen, M.L. Smith, and N. Filby, *School Class Size* (Beverly Hills, CA: Sage, 1982).

10. H.A. Averch, S.J. Carroll, T.S. Donaldson, H.J. Kiesling, and J. Pincus, *How Effective is Schooling? A Critical Review and Synthesis of Research Findings* (Santa Monica, CA: The Rand Corporation, 1972).

11. S.J. Carroll, "Search for Equity," in *Financing Education: Overcoming Inefficiency and Inequity*, edited by W.W. McMahon and T.G. Geske (Urbana, IL: University of Illinois Press, 1982). The second researcher is T.G. Geske, "Educational Finance Policy: A Search for Complementarities," *Educational Evaluation and*

Policy Analysis, Vol. 5 (1983), pp. 83-96.

12. E.A. Hanushek, "Throwing Money at Schools," *Journal of Policy Analysis and Management*, Volume 1, No. 1, pp. 17-27.

13. Herbert J. Walberg and William J. Fowler, Jr., "Expenditure and Size Efficiencies of Public School Districts."

14. Two excellent, in-depth profiles of Catholic schools in low-income neighborhoods (not only Chicago) are *Catholic High Schools: Their Impact on Low-Income Students*, produced by the National Catholic Educational Association; and *Inner-City Private Elementary Schools: A Study*, by Cibulka, O'Brien, and Zewe. Two excellent articles about Catholic schools are "Now Let Us Praise Catholic Schools," by Alfredo Lanier, *Chicago* magazine, October 1982; and "America's Best Run Schools," by Danielle L. Schultz, *The Washington Monthly*, November 1983.

15. Lanier, p. 153.

16. Archdiocese of Chicago, *Chicago Catholic Schools*, 1987-88 Edition.

17. Lanier.

18. James S. Coleman and Thomas Hoffer, *Public and Private High Schools: The Impact of Communities* (New York: Basic Books, 1987), p. xxiv.

19. Lanier.

20. Archdiocese of Chicago.

21. See Lanier; Cibulka, O'Brien, and Zewe; and Lillian Thomas, "Small Successes," *Reader* (Chicago), October 3, 1986.

22. U.S. Dept. of Education, Center for Education Statistics, *The Condition of Education*, 1987, p. 74.

23. David S. Seeley, a professor of education at the College of Staten Island, CUNY, observes: "Public school officials who complain about families abandoning public schools should ponder the degree to which they have contributed to the defection. School bureaucracies not only

do not seem to notice poor quality education but they also are often particularly deaf to the voice of those parents who are dissatisfied. These may well be the very parents who could contribute the most if listened to. They are also the most likely to leave if they feel there is no hope of response. School officials are often their own worst enemies when it comes to maintaining support for the public schools." *Education Through Partnership: Mediating Structures in Education* (Cambridge, MA: Ballinger Publishing Co., 1981).

24. The average Catholic elementary school in Chicago enrolls 350 students; the average high school enrolls 740. The systemwide average is 407 students per school. In the public schools, average elementary school enrollment is 600; the average public high school enrollment is 1,790. The systemwide average is 723.

25. For a full discussion, see Coleman and Hoffer, pp. 3-27. David Seeley finds that voluntary enrollment has the same positive effects on students: "The very act of selecting gives them a stake in the school they choose. Their choice represents an affirmation of their own values. Student behavior is often significantly transformed as a result, from rebellious or apathetic to cooperative and enthusiastic. Anyone observing this phenomenon will see that the process is one of affirmation, not just escape or negation." Seeley, *Education Through Partnership*.

26. Seeley.

27. Sociologist Morris Janowitz describes the diminishing influence of residential communities at some length in *The Last Half-Century: Society Change and Politics in America* (Chicago: University of Chicago Press, 1978), pp. 264-319. These insights are not new: Robert E. Park and Ernest W. Burgess, two founders of the Chicago school of urban sociology, described the process in *The City: Suggestions for*

Investigation of Human Behavior in the Urban Environment (Chicago: University of Chicago Press, 1925 (Midway Reprint, 1967)).

PART THREE

THE CURE

INTRODUCTION

> *We propose an idea in the great*
> *American Tradition: that you can*
> *increase excellence by increasing*
> *choice.*
>
> National Governors' Association
> *Time for Results*

We have documented the problems and short-comings of public schools in Chicago and the rest of the nation. We have come to understand the origins of these problems and why they often seem intractable. And we have examined schools that work, hoping to distill the lessons their successes can teach us. What remains to be found is a cure for Chicago's public school crisis.

We believe we have found the cure. It requires taking control of the schools from a remote and too-powerful bureaucracy and returning it to principals, teachers, and local community representatives. It requires giving the parents of students enrolled in each school a voice in the selection of its principal and the establishment of school policies. And it requires allowing parents to choose which schools their children attend.

In Chapters Eight and Nine, we present a school reform plan based on the concepts of voice and choice. The plan is the product of Chicagoans United to Reform Education (C.U.R.E.), a grassroots and interracial coalition of parents, teachers, businesspeople, and concerned citizens devoted to restructuring Chicago's schools. Michael J. Bakalis, a coauthor of this book, is cochairman of the C.U.R.E. coalition. This plan has generated widespread support and hope for eventual implementation.

In Chapters Ten and Eleven, we describe a reform that would go a step further. This plan, called Education Rebates, would build on the restructuring plan contained in the C.U.R.E. proposal but would guarantee good public schools by making the entire school system accountable to parents and to the community. Education Rebates would create a "bottom line" for public schools by allowing dissatisfied parents to withdraw their children from the public school system and reclaim part of their education taxes that otherwise would have gone to the public schools. Joseph L. Bast and Steven Baer, also coauthors of this book, are spokesmen for the Education Rebate plan.

Not all of the authors endorse all parts of the plans presented here. Mr. Bakalis believes the C.U.R.E. plan would bring effective and permanent reform without the Education Rebates described in the later chapters. Messrs. Bast and Baer believe the gains possible through C.U.R.E. will quickly be endangered unless Education Rebates are also passed. Mr. Walberg believes that both plans have merit and should be considered and possibly integrated with other plans put forward by the Board of Education, Chicago United, and other groups. These differences of opinion aside, we are united in our belief that the Chicago Public Schools can be improved. Moreover, we affirm that such an improvement is essential to the survival and prosperity of the city of Chicago itself.

In Chapter Twelve below, reform proposals put forward by the Chicago Teachers Union, the Mayor's

112

Education Summit, and the Chicago Partnership are summarized and discussed. The authors believe that there are valuable contributions to the reform debate to be found in each proposal, but only one, the Chicago Partnership proposal, addresses the underlying causes of the problems we have discussed. Unfortunately, the Chicago Partnership proposal is not a detailed plan, but only a series of "performance indicators" or goals for reform.

8

VOICE AND CHOICE: REAL REFORM

> *Essential to the restructuring of schools is providing individual schools with greater autonomy over the hiring of staff and the development of curriculum and greater responsibility for the educational performance of their students.*

> Committee for
>   Economic Development
> *Children in Need*

A Brief Summary of the C.U.R.E. Proposal

Real reform requires that parents and community members be given a genuine voice in the operations of their schools, and a choice of public schools in which to enroll their children. The C.U.R.E. plan would establish elected School Governing Councils in each school; mandate a reduction in the size and authority of the Board of Education administrative office; and (in the fifth year of the plan) allow parents to choose the public schools their children attend. The C.U.R.E. plan would reduce bureaucracy and create a "bottom-up" rather than "top-down" authority structure. It would produce quality schools for every Chicagoan.

The Origins of the C.U.R.E. Proposal

In early 1986, a small group of educators and community activists came together to explore ways to save a school system that seemed damaged almost beyond repair. Meeting informally at first, educators and members of community groups discussed the ingredients for a restructured and effective school system. A new umbrella organization was formed-- Chicagoans United to Reform Education -- and the acronym of the group, C.U.R.E., clearly expressed what they believed the sick Chicago Public Schools needed. Over time the coalition was enlarged, until by 1987 it had become a citywide group that not only was geographically representative, but also reflected the racial and socioeconomic diversity of Chicago.[1] Often having vastly different agendas and perspectives on other issues, this diverse group was united in its commitment to school reform in Chicago.

Over the two-year period 1986-88, the C.U.R.E. coalition engaged in systematic research on effective schools and urban education, consulted with experts from around the country, and involved community people from throughout Chicago in the process of creating a plan for school reform. From the beginning the coalition believed that a public school system so ineffective and unresponsive to change could not be saved through minor cosmetic "tinkering." Their final proposal reflects this conviction.

The C.U.R.E. plan is a unique, creative, far-reaching blueprint that would result in a total restructuring of Chicago's public schools. C.U.R.E. has offered such a strong prescription for school change because it believes the disease of the current system might well be fatal if left unattended.

Old Ideas in a New Setting

The key ingredients of the C.U.R.E. proposal are school governance through local elections and choice of schools, division of authority among different elected bodies, and parental choice within the public school system. These are not new or radical ideas.

Local control by elected school councils is in fact the norm throughout Illinois. The Illinois Department of Tourism once used the slogan, "Outside Chicago, there's a place called Illinois." The purpose of the slogan was to encourage those living in other states, as well as Chicagoans, to recognize the attractions of the entire state. It was a clever and appropriate approach because even for residents of Chicago, "downstate" Illinois is often a mystery. Chicagoans could learn a great deal from the way the rest of Illinois operates its public schools.

Not all Illinois schools outside Chicago are excellent, but overall student achievement levels and citizen satisfaction are far higher than in Chicago. While few of these communities face the socioeconomic problems that confront inner-city schools in Chicago, even with these differences the ineffectiveness of Chicago's schools is striking.

Outside Chicago, Illinois is home to one of the most decentralized public education systems in America. Almost 1,000 school districts (of which the city of Chicago is one) dot the state, and each one, with the exception of Chicago, is governed by an elected board of community citizens. Through this elective process, downstate board members must go to their communities for support and are, in turn, accountable to them. A community unhappy with local school policy has access to its board members and ultimately can dismiss them by not supporting their re-election.

Elected boards of education in Illinois hire and fire principals and teachers, help determine curriculum, and decide how money will be spent. This does not mean that these board members always make wise decisions, but in each case the decisions are their own -- they have no one else to blame. In many respects, they own and direct their community schools. Perhaps of greatest importance is that such direct democratic control is most often found in small settings. Of the nearly one thousand Illinois school districts, 750 serve fewer students than are served by the *average Chicago high school*.

A second important idea behind the C.U.R.E. plan is also one very old in America and one proven to be successful -- the specific division and assignment of governing powers to different levels of government. In the national/state relationship it is called federalism, while in Illinois our state constitution delegates certain powers to state government and allows localities to exercise certain other powers.

In both our government structures and in the C.U.R.E. proposal the assumptions behind the division of responsibilities are the same: some tasks are accomplished more effectively through a larger scale, more centralized approach while others can be more appropriately accomplished at the local level. Control also is built in when power is divided rather than concentrated -- power divided is power held in check. Here too, these very old and very American concepts are at the core of the C.U.R.E. proposal.

A third well-tested idea embodied in the C.U.R.E approach is choice. As we saw in Chapter Four, choice in education has a long and distinguished history in America. Educator David S. Seeley has said that "Choice is indeed not at all new in American education. It was traditional until centralized,

118

bureaucratic, and governmental schooling became dominant."[2] In Chicago, choice exists today for the many thousands of parents who choose to enroll their children in private schools, or who can afford to move to neighborhoods with better public schools. While the idea of choice is not new, making it an option for *every* family is.

The heart of the C.U.R.E. plan is not a radical, new approach to school structure, governance, and organization. It is instead a set of ideas that are solidly founded in history, tradition, and current practice. It is, in fact, merely a group of old ideas proposed for a new setting -- the City of Chicago.

Overview of the C.U.R.E Plan

The C.U.R.E. proposal is a carefully structured and detailed approach to school reform in Chicago. Though essentially complete, some parts of the plan were still being developed at the time this book was published, and some changes might be made as the plan moves toward adoption by the Illinois General Assembly. Although a general overview of the plan will be presented here, the full impact of its changes can be understood only by studying the detailed plan. Instructions on how to obtain a copy of the plan appear at the end of this book.

The C.U.R.E. plan is directed at "debureaucratizing" the Chicago Public Schools. As in all classic bureaucratic models, decisions in the current school structure emanate from the top down through multiple layers of administration to reach individual schools and the children. The plan turns this process upside down, with the most important decisions originating at the most local level -- the individual *school* -- and working upward to the central authority. At the same time, for efficiency, a few decision-making powers remain centrally held and exert influence down to the individual schools. This change in the flow of power is illustrated below.

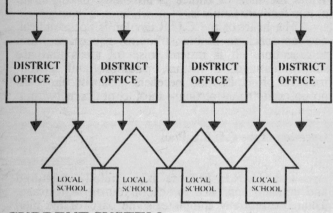

CURRENT SYSTEM

C.U.R.E. PLAN

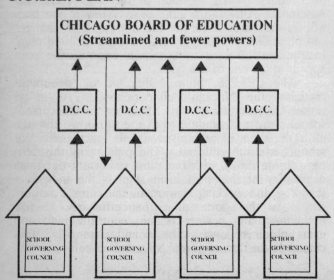

The key to the C.U.R.E. plan and the focus of its attention is the *individual school*. Here the most important decisions that directly affect learning will be made by a responsible principal and an *elected* body with real decision-making authority -- the School Governing Council. This council will consist of nineteen members, six of whom are parents of children enrolled in the Chicago Public Schools, six teachers, six adult community members without children enrolled in the schools, and the principal. The councils will have power over the hiring and firing of principals and teachers, the allocation of money, and the establishment of curriculum (within systemwide guidelines). Thus, accountability is created at the level closest to the student, parent, and taxpayer.

The C.U.R.E. plan gives school principals an authority and responsibility they currently do not have in Chicago public schools. C.U.R.E. assures that principals are not only administrators with power to manage the school, but also that they assume the role of *instructional* leaders. They must provide the leadership in developing the specifics of the school's curriculum and learning programs as mandated by the School Governing Council. Further, the principal's role is enhanced by the ability to select staff, and accountability is assured by having principals hired on a contractual basis by the council.

To ensure that the individual School Governing Councils communicate and cooperate where savings or efficiencies could be accomplished, the C.U.R.E. plan calls for the creation of district coordinating councils (DCCs). Each DCC would be responsible to approximately thirty schools and would explore ways the schools could work together or with the larger community to achieve educational goals.

The district coordinating councils should not be viewed as an additional bureaucratic layer, since membership will consist of one representative from each school governing council and each DCC will have only one staff person. Further, each DCC will

121

CENTRAL BOARD

Powers:
Negotiate collective bargaining agreement
Allocate funds to schools by formula
Purchasing
Protect individual rights
Conduct research
Set school boundaries
Oversee special education
Hire chancellor

Membership:
11 members appointed by mayor from slate provided
by School Board Review Commission

DISTRICT COORDINATING COUNCIL
(one paid facilitator)

Powers:
Foster communication and cooperation among schools
Elect School Board Review Commission

Membership:
Member from each School Governing Council in
district. (Must be parent or community member.)

LOCAL SCHOOL/SCHOOL GOVERNING COUNCIL

Powers:
Develop school improvement plan
Hire and fire principal
Approve teacher hiring
Set curriculum policy
Control physical plant and ground
Prepare and approve school budget

Membership:
Six parents, elected by parents in the school
Six teachers, elected by teachers in the school
Six community members, elected by community

operate on a budget contributed by its member schools. These DCCs will also elect members of the School Board Review Commission, the body that nominates candidates for the Board of Education to the mayor.

While the C.U.R.E. proposal gives most important powers to the school governing council and the school principal, other powers are exercised by a Central Board of Education, in accordance with the division of powers principle. This board, composed of members nominated by the School Board Review Commission and appointed by the mayor of Chicago, will have the following principal responsibilities: allocating funds to individual school governing councils based on a formula set by law, negotiating collective bargaining agreements, overseeing individual school budgets and payments of funds, purchasing supplies, overseeing special education and desegregation programs, administering building maintenance, and hiring a Chief Administrator.

The duties of the central board are significant, but they are primarily in the areas of administrative services, oversight, and support. Thus, the real authority to affect learning remains at the individual school. The chart below illustrates the membership and powers of the central board, the district coordinating councils, and the school governing councils.

C.U.R.E recognizes the scope and complexity of the changes it proposes, and thus its plan calls for a three-year transition period to move the school system from its current structure to the new model in an orderly fashion.

Voice and Choice in the Schools

Provisions that given parents and taxpayers a say in how schools are managed evident throughout the C.U.R.E. proposal. Individuals currently denied a voice in their schools may campaign for school governing council positions or obtain direct access to the school decision makers *at their local school*. Real participation is possible in curriculum selection, expenditure of money, and the hiring and firing of teachers.

Voice is assured by the procedure for selecting members of the central board. Recommendations for appointment to the central board come from the grassroots upward, from communities to the district coordinating council and then to the mayor, who must select from among the names recommended. At every level the new school system has multiple points of citizen input and checks on those decisions that parents and the community believe are not in the best interest of the children.

The power of choice is held by the elected School Governing Council, which hires the school principal and has final approval over the choice of teachers for the school. Within the limits of the law, the councils can make choices in curriculum matters and in the planning and expenditure of their budgetary allocation. They also can choose to give, or to withhold, authority and money to the district coordinating council. The DCCs choose by election the committee that nominates the slate of candidates from which the mayor appoints the central board.

And most importantly, parents specifically are given the power of choice. Parents may apply for their child's admission to any Chicago public school. If the number of applicants to a school exceeds the space available, students will be selected by lottery, not by test results. This provision, which would go into effect in the fifth year of the plan, would be modeled after successful choice programs in Minnesota, Massachusetts, and New York's District Four.[3] Thus, a competitive ingredient is installed to allow consumer choice not available under the current system.

Conclusion

It would be foolish to claim that this restructuring of the Chicago Public Schools would immediately result in massive numbers of student success stories. Many other variables both within and especially outside the school remain powerful obstacles to educational achievement. The influence of community disorganization, poverty, divided families, street crime, and violence will not disappear because the opportunities for input and decision making are made available in Chicago's schools. But to the extent that concerned parents and citizens seek to shape their own lives and those of their children, they should be given the opportunity to do so. What is clear is that we no longer can afford to do nothing.

There is strong evidence that the changes proposed by the C.U.R.E plan can result in a vastly improved, workable system appropriate to a large urban area. This is a realistic plan, incorporating the experiences and lessons of successful schools and school systems. It has been produced by an unprecedented grassroots coalition of black, white, and Hispanic parents and concerned citizens. It deserves a fair hearing and a chance to succeed.

1. As of this writing, the C.U.R.E. coalition consists of: Center for New Horizons; Designs for Change; Loyola University of Chicago, School of Education; Near North Development Corporation, People's Coalition for Educational Reform; and Save Our Neighborhoods/Save Our City Coalition (SON/SOC). These community groups are themselves often coalitions of other organizations.

2. David S. Seeley, *Education Through Partnership: Mediating Structures in Education* (Cambridge, MA: Ballinger Publishing Co., 1981).

3. Massachusetts has seventy-one public schools of choice in nine communities enrolling over 37,000 students. See Ross Zerchykov, "A Context Note: Choice, Diversity and Desegregation in Massachusetts," *Equity and Choice*, nd, pp. 9-18. Recent proposals call for extending choice to all parents with children in the Boston public schools. See William Snider, "Allow Parents to Choose Schools, Boston Task Force Recommends," *Education Week*, April 1, 1987, p. 9. Concerning Minnesota's choice programs, see Ted Kolderie, "School Improvement and the Dynamics of Choice," *Public Services Redesign Project*, July 1985; and "Choice for the New Generation?" *Reason*, June 1988, p. 16. For a description of New York City's District Four, see Janet R. Price and Jane R. Stern, "Magnet Schools as a Strategy for Integration and School Reform," *Yale Law and Policy Review*, Vol. 5, No. 2, Spring/Summer 1987, pp. 309ff.

9

VOICE AND CHOICE: TEN QUESTIONS AND ANSWERS

Attempts to put more money into strengthening an old, standardized system won't work.

Mario Fantini
Dean, School of Education
University of Massachusetts

1. **Hasn't school decentralization been tried before and failed?**

The word "decentralization" calls forth different definitions and sometimes confusing images in people's minds. Decentralization can take many shapes and forms, but in its simplest sense all of the schools in Illinois outside Chicago are decentralized. The evidence presented in Chapter Four showing that

127

smaller districts outperform large districts is proof of how well decentralization works.

The term "decentralization" has also been used in reference to a policy put into place in large urban school systems. Probably the most famous example is New York City, but decentralization has also been tried in other major cities, including Detroit and Los Angeles. The experience of Detroit was not satisfactory, and eventually the schools returned to a centralized system. The history of urban education in this country reveals that cities have very often alternated between centralized and decentralized systems.

Decentralization in New York City meant moving authority and responsibility to district-level administrators. School-based governance and mechanisms for parental involvement, essential components of the C.U.R.E. plan, were not implemented in New York. For this reason, the success or failure of "decentralization" in New York City should be used to predict the odds of success or failure for the C.U.R.E. plan.

New York City's experience with decentralization has been thoroughly debated, and one can find examples of both success and failure depending when and where one looks at that system. Undoubtedly there have been examples of failure, corruption, and union control of the decision-making process in some areas of New York. However, this should not detract from the overall assessment of the New York experience, which is, by and large, very positive.

The research regarding the benefits of decentralization, increased parent involvement, and school site governance presents a picture of school systems that can work and, perhaps for the first time, offer quality urban education. Only 34 percent of New York's elementary school students scored above the national average on reading achievement tests in 1971. During seventeen years of decentralization, reading achievement levels for elementary students climbed steadily, so that by 1987, 63 percent were reading above the national average. This gain was realized despite the fact that during the 1971-1987 period, one-third of the white students left the school system, severe staff reductions were implemented, and procedures used to test student achievement were improved.[1]

David Rogers' comprehensive analysis of the New York decentralization experience concludes that it has created social peace, helped shape the schools into a legitimate community institution, made educational goals more compatible with community desires, and encouraged greater creativity and efficiency.[2]

Weaknesses within the New York system also offer some valuable lessons for Chicago. For example, the size of New York's community school districts makes election extremely difficult without a large campaign fund or the support of the unions or the Democratic Party.[3] C.U.R.E. has addressed these issues by moving decision making to the local school level, rather than dividing Chicago into districts similar to those in New York.

2. Isn't it unrealistic to expect poor or uneducated parents to effectively run a school?

Perhaps the best way to approach this concern is to realize that in every other district in Illinois, except Chicago, we allow people to make these very same kinds of decisions. The individuals who run their schools in these other districts are not all middle class or wealthy, nor are they all college or even high school graduates. And yet they do come together in small communities, campaign for school board positions, and become involved in important school decisions. Further, this process goes on in more than 90 percent of the school districts throughout this country.

It is also important to remember that no special knowledge or experience is required for people to participate and vote in the elections of their state representative, governor, president, or alderman.

Can we have faith in the ability of people to make decisions pertaining to the federal budget, foreign policy, and the direction of the country, yet not trust their judgment in matters pertaining to the direction of the schools within their own community?

The fact is that parents who participate in educational governance use common sense when addressing the development and continuance of school policy. Simply because people are poor does not mean they are incapable. Like their more affluent or more educated fellow parents, low-income people, for the most part, care very much about their community, their schools, and certainly their children. And just as we have faith in the overwhelming majority of citizens throughout this state who help manage their local public school, so must we have faith that parents in Chicago will make the right decisions when given the appropriate training and the opportunity to do so.

Attendance at school board meetings and school board election turnouts in Illinois, and the rest of the country, are rarely high. And yet, there are always small groups of people who do participate and who are interested enough to make a real contribution. The C.U.R.E. plan calls for the participation of only six parents and six community members from each school neighborhood. That seems like a very conservative and reasonable requirement. In the past, people in Chicago have been discouraged from participating in school governance because they often knew it was a sham and their ideas would not be taken seriously or acted upon.

3. What would the C.U.R.E. plan mean to teachers?

The C.U.R.E. plan provides for teacher input and would allow teachers more participation in school management than anywhere else in Illinois. C.U.R.E. believes it is important that teachers, as trained professionals, be given the opportunity to affect and

130

help shape the educational program of their schools. For too long, education has operated on a confrontational model in which school boards and teachers acted as antagonists.

For a very long time, teachers have said they want to guide and direct their profession and to have a voice in shaping the teaching-learning process. We believe this is not only a reasonable request but a matter of critical importance to the quality of education. Certainly the growth of employee participation occurring today within the private sector ought to be a positive example of what can happen when workers are given an opportunity to participate in the decision-making process. We consider such involvement to be a positive step, one that ought to be taken in the school environment as well.

While we encourage teacher participation, we do not want to repeat the negative experiences of New York. Thus under our plan, teachers will not be able to control School Governing Councils because they are given only one-third of the votes on that body. The remaining two-thirds will be controlled by parents and other community members. Further, teachers would not participate in the negotiation of their own contracts and benefits, since that process will be carried out by the central board, which does not have teachers as members. We think that our plan offers an excellent opportunity for teachers to participate, but not to dominate.

4. **Would the C.U.R.E. plan cause chaos and confusion by allowing each school to adopt its own curriculum and programs?**

There is substantial diversity in public education throughout the country and throughout Illinois. The State of Illinois does not force the state's one thousand school districts to adopt a uniform curriculum or specific teaching objectives or outcomes.

As we saw in Chapter Three, individual schools in the Chicago Public Schools system have limited freedom to tailor curriculum to their communities' interests and needs. The C.U.R.E. proposal protects this individual school autonomy by establishing it as public policy, and seeks to give parents and community members a larger role in school-based decisions.

To ensure that diversity does not turn into chaos, every Chicago public school, like all other schools in this state, will have to meet state requirements. For example, a school district or school site may not decide to eliminate instruction of American history and replace it with basket-weaving. Such deviations from curriculum requirements are forbidden under state law. School Governing Councils, however, would be allowed to decide their goals and objectives and choose materials to meet them.

The C.U.R.E. plan would allow a council to select a teaching sequence it believes best for its students, decide when courses are to be offered, and choose which special programs are needed for its school. In other words, the C.U.R.E. plan allows some creativity and some choice in curriculum planning. Educational diversity offers a very healthy learning alternative.

5. Will the C.U.R.E. plan save money or cost more?

The major reason to restructure the Chicago Public Schools is not to save money (or to obtain more state funds), but to improve the quality of educational services they provide. The C.U.R.E. plan should be enacted because it will give people a real voice in determining what quality education means and how best to achieve it.

Adoption of the C.U.R.E. plan would result in some cost savings and some new costs. We estimate that reducing the bureaucracy at the district and

132

field offices will save taxpayers $11.3 million each year.[4] Downsizing and streamlining the central administration will save an additional $12.5 million each year. But countervailing these cost reductions would be spending increases in these areas:

A **School Improvement Incentives Fund** for salary bonuses and educational opportunities to reward school staffs who make significant progress toward learning objectives;

Additional funds for schools serving low-income students through the **closing of loopholes** in the state Title I law;

Capital improvements to bring all school buildings up to minimum standards;

School Improvement Discretionary Funds for each school;

Training for School Governing Council members;

Administration of School Governing Council **elections**.

Our best estimates of the *net* added cost of C.U.R.E. are $25.3 million in the first year, $2.4 million in the second year, $12.5 million in the third year, and $23 million in the fourth year.[5] The experience of Minnesota, which has implemented an aggressive program of choice and local school autonomy within the public school system, suggests that adoption of these policies need not raise costs. Minnesota Governor Rudy Perpich and Commissioner of Education Ruth Randall have said that the promise of long-term efficiency gains makes local school governance and choice consistent with the demands of fiscal austerity.[6]

6. **Will some poor city schools suffer because their local revenue collection will be much less than that collected in the more affluent parts of the city?**

The C.U.R.E. plan does not call for local sub-districts to raise their own money. In a city like Chicago, where economic resources vary greatly from neighborhood to neighborhood, such a process would be chaotic and inequitable. Under the C.U.R.E. plan, all monies collected from local, state, and federal sources will be turned over to the Central Administration, as they are today. The board will allocate funds to individual School Governing Councils based on a formula that will be set forth in the law. That formula will take into account special conditions of individual schools, such as the level of poverty, the number of special education students, and other factors. Each school will receive a sum of money based upon this formula, and each School Governing Council will have the discretion, within the boundaries of the law, to spend that money as it believes best. To ensure accountability, the central board will monitor individual school budgets and payments.

7. **Does the elective process put forth in the C.U.R.E. plan open up the school system to corruption, patronage, and control by political parties in Chicago?**

While there are always risks in a democratic process, the C.U.R.E. plan assumes Chicagoans are as intelligent, honest, moral, and conscientious as their fellow citizens who participate in similar processes throughout the state and the nation. Still, there are numerous checks against external political manipulation built into the C.U.R.E. program. These checks come from both central board oversight of the

School Governing Councils and, perhaps most importantly, from election of representatives.

Under the C.U.R.E. proposal, individuals who promote policies that seem unfair or dishonest can be eliminated from their School Governing Council through the elective process. While this process may not be perfect, it works reasonably well in every other sector where people are elected. Schools will be prey to political maneuvering no more than other institutions. We believe it is a mistake to think that the democratic process should not be involved in education.

Ultimately we stand on the principle that people must have faith in the citizenry, in their honesty, in their integrity, and in their good intentions. As they have in both the public sector and the private sector, abuses undoubtedly will occur. But we believe that the potential for a quality school system in which every child has a chance to learn far outweighs the risks imposed by adults who sometimes stray from proper behavior.

8. Has this plan been tried, or been successful, anywhere else in the United States?

The C.U.R.E. plan is a new, comprehensive approach to school governance. Although an exact replica of our plan does not currently exist in any school district or major school system in the country, the plan is founded upon careful and systematic research of those elements that make up an effective school governance system. Certain elements of our plan, including the choice component, are working effectively in school systems around the nation and in other countries.[7] We are presenting a new vision for Chicago that we believe can be a model for the rest of the nation.

Very often, extreme conditions call for new and creative approaches. It is clear to those involved in the C.U.R.E plan that the Chicago Public Schools are

135

in need of very comprehensive and even radical reform. Because we think the alternatives -- either "tinkering" with the system, which will result only in cosmetic change, or leaving the system alone -- are entirely unacceptable, we believe we must act quickly and boldly before we lose another generation of students.

9. What new opportunities for voice will Chicago residents have under the C.U.R.E. plan?

The citizens of Chicago currently have almost no voice in the operation and governance of the Chicago Public Schools. Chicago residents and parents of children in school cannot voice their opinion on the membership of the school board. Nor do they have authority over who will be the principal of their school or which teachers will be assigned to their school. Today, they have no voice whatsoever in curriculum, in the delivery of educational services, or in the expenditure of funds for individual schools. In other words, they are currently shut out of the process.

Under the C.U.R.E. plan, many of these powers are given to elected officials at the local school level. By voting for these officials, all Chicago residents will be given real decision-making input. C.U.R.E. does not offer some sham advisory council on which the members' advice may or may not be taken. Rather, C.U.R.E. offers a true input process, established and enforceable by law. The C.U.R.E. plan empowers the people in the city to control the schools they own.

10. What choice will Chicago residents have under the C.U.R.E. plan that they do not have now?

The C.U.R.E. plan allows people to choose the persons who will run the school in their community. Their elected representives then have the authority to choose a principal, select teachers, determine curriculum, choose textbooks, approve or disapprove a budget, and to make other choices. C.U.R.E. also gives School Governing Councils a choice of school structure, such as whether classrooms will be organized on an open class model, or whether schools will select a more traditional closed classroom approach. And unlike the present system, people representing local schools can nominate persons for the school board.

Parents will also be allowed to choose where their children go to school. Under the C.U.R.E. plan, a competitive public school system is established. Public schools will have to perform effectively or parents may opt to take their children out of the ineffective school and place them in another, better public school. This kind of choice will put the burden on the school to be as good as it can be, or to go out of business. In those extreme cases where a particularly low-quality school loses so many students it cannot remain open, the principal and teachers would not automatically be transferred elsewhere; rather, the individuals who worked in that unproductive school would have to find new jobs. We believe this degree of choice is absolutely essential to assuring accountability within the public school system. This degree of choice is not available in any other major urban public school system.

1. Office of Educational Assessment of New York City Board of Education, *Reading Achievement of Students in New York City Public Schools, Grades Two Through Nine, 1971-87*, 1987.
2. David Rogers and Norman H. Chung, *110 Lingston Street Revisited: Decentralization in Action* (New York: New York University Press, 1983).
3. Manhattan Borough President's Task Force on Education and Decentralization, *Improving the Odds: Making Decentralization Work for Children* (New York: President of the Borough of Manhattan, 1987).
4. C.U.R.E., *Cost Analysis of the C.U.R.E. Plan, a Year-by-Year Estimate of Added Costs and Savings*, April 11, 1988.
5. Ibid.
6. William Snider, "The Call for Choice," *Education Week*, June 24, 1987, p. C23.
7. See endnote three for Chapter Nine for references. For descriptions of how choice works in other countries, see Edward Ignas, Raymond J. Corsini, et al., *Comparative Educational Systems* (Itasca, IL: F.E. Peacock Publishers, Inc., 1981). In particular, note the essay on West German education by Dr. Hans Schieser.

10

TUITION REBATES: ONE STEP FURTHER

Accountability and responsiveness in public education cannot be legislated, regulated, or achieved by fiat or good intentions alone. They require both incentives and disincentives. The system that best meets these objectives fairly, efficiently, and rapidly is a market system.

Committee for
Economic Development
Investing in Our Children

A Brief Summary of Education Rebates

Education Rebates would guarantee quality public education by extending choice to the poor and to those whose tax dollars fund the Chicago Public Schools. Education Rebates reduce the tax penalty imposed on parents who remove their children from low-quality or unresponsive public schools. They also allow taxpayers to choose which schools they wish to support. Education Rebates guarantee good public schools by creating a bottom line for the public school system and by truly empowering parents and community members.

Is C.U.R.E. enough?

Adoption of the C.U.R.E. plan to restructure public school administration in Chicago will be a major step toward improvement of the Chicago Public Schools. By moving important decisions down to the school level, the plan ends the concentration of authority that fosters a large and unresponsive bureaucracy. By allowing parents to choose the public schools in which they will enroll their children, the C.U.R.E. plan starts to remove the negative effects of geographical assignment of children to schools.

Would the C.U.R.E. plan, by itself, correct the structural problems described in Part Two of this book? The hope behind the plan is that local governance and choice will assure efficiency and responsiveness to parents' and students' demands. But what of the missing bottom line, the perverse incentives of a bureaucracy, and the superior organizing abilities of public employees, all of which were discussed in Chapter Five? Does the C.U.R.E. plan hold the public school *system* accountable to parents, or does it only allow parents to select among many low-quality, still bureaucratized schools?

The C.U.R.E. plan contains many checks and balances aimed at preventing it from falling victim to the bureaucracy that has such a hold on the current school system. But one additional reform would *guarantee* that the benefits of decentralized administration would be realized and protected: Education Rebates.

Allowing choice *within* the public school system creates some competitive pressure on low-quality schools, but it does not guarantee that the public school system as a whole will be competitive with nonpublic schools in the city. In short, the entire public school *system* is not made to compete for students or revenue.

Under the C.U.R.E. plan, members of the central board will still make critically important funding and management decisions. Board members still will be protected from the consequences of mistakes made by its central and local management because parents who wish to enroll their children in more effective nonpublic schools face a stiff penalty for doing so. This is because the C.U.R.E. plan leaves in place the penalty of having to pay twice for nonpublic education -- taxes to support the schools that no longer serve them, and tuition at the schools to which they flee.

Legislation to decentralize administration may restore some accountability and diversity to the public schools. But so long as parents must send their children to public schools or face paying twice for the education of their children, the public schools will remain protected from parental dissatisfaction. The current system penalizes concerned parents who exercise their most effective sanction against poor quality: withdrawal of their children from the system. It thereby reduces the clout of parents in a way that nonpublic schools cannot. So long as this difference exists, the benefits of local school governance are in danger of being lost.

Education Rebates would reduce the penalty imposed on parents who remove their children from dangerous or low-quality public schools. Very simply, an Education Rebate is a way for the government to *give back* some of the education taxes paid by persons who voluntarily pay for a child's educational expenses. Since these persons are freeing the gov-

141

ernment of its obligation to finance the child's education, they would be entitled to receive some of the tax dollars that would otherwise have gone to the child's education.

Low-income families would benefit most from reducing the tax penalty on choice because they typically cannot afford to pay both taxes *and* tuition. Upper-income families have always had some choice of schools for their children because they can afford to pay the penalty. The main advantage of abolishing the tax penalty is that it would give low- and middle-income families the same freedom of choice that more wealthy families now enjoy.[1]

It is important to understand that the purpose of an Education Rebate program is *not* to harm the public schools. The purpose is just the opposite: to guarantee good public schools by restoring accountability to parents and other community members. Because Education Rebates would reimburse parents for some or all of the cost of enrolling a child in a nonpublic school, such a program would remove existing financial barriers that some families face, but would not make it profitable for a parent to withdraw his or her child from a public school.

Education Rebates would benefit public schools in a second way: parents who make contributions to *public* schools also would qualify for a rebate; public schools would be encouraged to compete for contributions from parents and community representatives, once again making them more responsive and accountable.

For Education Rebates to be effective, it is not necessary that any parents actually choose to remove their children from the Chicago Public Schools. It is sufficient that teachers and administrators know that any parent -- not just the wealthy or well-educated ones -- *can* leave the system. This creates a systemwide "bottom line" that has hitherto been missing in the public schools.

Kinds of Tax Relief Defined

The literature on tax relief for parents who voluntarily contribute to the education of a child generally speaks of *tax credits* and *tax deductions*. There are important differences between the two, and a *tax rebate* is still another form of tax relief. Let's quickly define these terms.

Tax deductions are subtracted from our taxable income before we figure what we owe. For example, we are claiming a deduction when we subtract a "personal exemption" of $1,900 from our income on federal income tax forms. By lowering our income, the tax deduction lowers our tax liability. But a $1,900 tax deduction does not lower the amount of taxes we owe by $1,900. It lowers it by a lesser amount (the amount of the deduction times the tax rate). Minnesota and Iowa both allow tax deductions for educational expenses.

A *tax credit* is different. It directly reduces the amount we pay in taxes by the full amount of the credit. For example, if before the credit we owed $500 in taxes, and the credit were for $300, then after the credit we only owe $200. A $300 tax credit means paying $300 less in taxes. A tax credit plan for educational expenses is being considered in California.

A *tax rebate* is different from either a deduction or a credit, because it recognizes that many lower income people pay taxes indirectly, without having any *formal* tax liability. Poor people pay taxes when property taxes and corporate income taxes are passed on to them in the form of higher rent by their landlords. Tax rebates are a form of tax relief that does not exclude the poor from its benefits. With rebates aimed at helping the poor, it is even possible for a rebate to exceed the amount of a poor person's *de facto* tax liability: this is called a subsidized rebate.

Two other elements of the vocabulary of tax relief are *relief ceilings* (or maximum allowed amounts) and *relief floors* (or minimum amounts for which all taxpayers would automatically qualify). For example, if a family qualified for $2,000 in tax relief but the *relief ceiling* was $1,000, then the family would be entitled to only $1,000. Conversely, if a family qualified for only $100 in tax relief but a *relief floor* of $300 existed, then the family would qualify for $300. Relief ceilings and floors allow us to tailor tax relief so that everyone receives some benefit from the program.

An Education Rebate Plan

Though a tax rebate plan for educational expenses could take many forms, one plan seems superior to all the rest. This plan is the **Renters and Homeowners Education Rebate Plan**. This plan, like the C.U.R.E. plan, was still being refined when this book went to press.

As its name implies, the Renters and Homeowners Education Tax Rebate plan (or the Education Rebate plan for short) provides tax rebates to both homeowners and renters. Here are the main components of the plan:

Anyone who contributes to the educational expenses of a child at a registered nonpublic or public school in Chicago will qualify for an Education Rebate. More than one person may contribute toward the educational expenses of any particular child.

For **renters** in Chicago, the amount of the Education Rebate is the lesser of school property taxes passed on to them by their landlord in the form of rent, the amount paid in education expenses that year, or $1,000. A relief floor of $300 will be established, so that regardless of the amount of property taxes indirectly paid through rent, every family can claim a tax credit for the amount of educational expenses paid up to $300.

144

For **homeowners** in Chicago, the amount of the Education Rebate is the lesser of property taxes paid to the Board of Education, the amount paid in qualifying education expenses that year, or $1,000. Regardless of the amount of property taxes paid, every family can claim a tax credit for the amount of actual educational expenses paid up to $300.

Businesses in Chicago also qualify for Education Rebates equal to the amount contributed to a registered public or nonpublic school, but not to exceed ten percent of the amount of property taxes paid to the Board of Education.

Application forms for Education Rebates, together with receipts for qualifying education expenses or contributions, will be delivered to qualifying persons by the schools receiving financial support. Homeowners will mail the completed forms to the Cook County Treasurer's Office, which will confirm the information provided by the applicant and issue a rebate check based on the formula described above. Renters will follow the same procedure, but will also request an education tax receipt from their landlords and will send that completed form along with their application to the Cook County Treasurer.

Why the lesser amount?

The reader will immediately notice that the maximum Education Rebate is determined by the *lesser* of school taxes paid and the amount of actual spending on educational expenses. Why was this formula chosen? The explanation has two parts.

First, if education taxes paid are *less* than the cost of educational expenses paid voluntarily, then it is proper that the rebate be in the amount of taxes paid, not actual expenses. The reason is that the penalty currently imposed on parents who enroll their children in nonpublic schools is not the cost of

145

nonpublic tuition but the taxes they pay, directly or indirectly, for school services they do not use. Parents should not be forced to pay for schools that fail to provide a level of service acceptable to them. But by the same token, *taxpayers* have no obligation to pay the full tuition at whatever school to which parents send their children instead. So relief should be sufficient to eliminate the tax penalty but not necessarily pay the complete cost of the replacement school's tuition.

The second part of the explanation concerns the situation where education taxes are *more* than the amount voluntarily paid on educational expenses. Shouldn't the parents be awarded "relief sufficient to eliminate the tax penalty," rather than the lesser amount actually spent on educational expenses? Perhaps the most ethical answer is, "Yes, they should be." But many people believe this would lead to a decrease in overall spending on education, as persons who don't have children enrolled in the public schools could make token contributions to the schools and then ask for their entire education tax payments back as rebates. To avoid this we say that people are entitled to relief from the tax penalty only if they voluntarily spend a comparable amount on educational services provided by either public or nonpublic schools. This way, the total amount of money being spent on education remains the same or increases, while the public schools do not face as great a threat of a sudden revenue loss. Limiting Education Rebates to the lesser of taxes paid or actual spending on educational services provides an important protection for the public schools. If Education Rebates were for the full amount of tuition at nonpublic schools, more parents would be moved to enroll their children at expensive schools against which the public schools might not be able to compete.

146

To understand how the Education Rebate program would work, it is best to start with a description of how renters would qualify for the program.

Though many people don't realize it, renters pay property taxes. Landlords view property taxes as one of many costs of doing business -- like water bills, maintenance, insurance, and the like -- and pass them along to the tenants in the form of higher rent. Each time a tenant pays rent, then, he or she is actually paying a property tax.

Because renters pay the school property taxes indirectly, a procedure is needed to allow them to calculate their rebates. A landlord's property tax bill, like the individual homeowner's bill, clearly indicates what share of the total bill is going to the Board of Education. Provided with a formula that distributes total property taxes among the tenants occupying apartments in their buildings, it would be a simple matter for landlords to make the necessary calculations and provide the information to their tenants upon request.[2] The Education Rebate plan would require landlords to provide their tenants with this information if asked, and would provide landlords with the necessary forms.

A renter who pays all or part of a child's educational expenses could apply for an Education Rebate by requesting just two short forms: an Education Tax Receipt from his landlord and a Renters Application Form from the school he supported. On the second form, he would indicate the total amount of qualifying educational expenses, how much his landlord estimates he paid indirectly in education property taxes, and the rebate he is entitled to. The form, together with the Education Tax Receipt and receipts documenting educational expenses, would be delivered to the Cook County Treasurer's Office, where the Treasurer's staff would confirm the calculations and issue the Education Rebate check.

Under the Education Rebate program, every renter who pays all or part of the educational expenses of a child attending a public or nonpublic school located in Chicago would be entitled to a rebate. The amount of the rebate would be equal to the amount of educational expenses actually paid *or* the amount of taxes paid to the Board of Education, whichever is less. There would be a relief ceiling of $1,000 per year on the rebate that could be claimed, and a relief floor of $300 or educational expenses actually paid, whichever is less. The rationale for these specific numbers will be presented below.

Some renters will find that their landlords paid very little in property taxes, and in the absence of a relief floor they would qualify for very small rebates. This is particularly true of low-income families and families occupying public housing. (The Chicago Housing Authority does not pay property taxes on its residential units, so people living in CHA buildings would have no property taxes to report at all.) The minimum Education Rebate of $300 or actual spending on education, whichever is less, ensures that they will benefit from the program.

Homeowners

The program would work in a similar fashion for Chicago homeowners. Currently, every homeowner in Chicago pays property taxes that are earmarked for the Chicago Board of Education. These taxes are clearly identified on the homeowner's tax notice received each year from the Cook County Treasurer's Office.

Applying for the Education Rebate would be simple. The homeowner would request a receipt and a Homeowner's Application Form from the school that received his payments or contributions during the year. The homeowner would then record the total amount of qualifying expenditures, record the amount paid in school property taxes from the previous year, and indicate the rebate amount requested. The form would be delivered to the Cook County Treasurer's Office, where the information would be confirmed and a check issued.

Businesses

Today, businesses pay approximately 50 percent of the total amount of property taxes received by the Chicago Board of Education. Though they foot a large part of the bill, businesses have no voice in the operation of the schools.

Allowing businesses to choose which schools they wish to support would encourage the public schools to listen more closely to the concerns of the business community, and conversely will give the business community a greater reason to pay attention to the public schools. Since contributions to public as well as nonpublic schools would qualify a firm for a tax rebate, principals and parents would have strong incentives to communicate with their local business communities.

The purpose of the Education Rebate program, as was stressed before, is not to harm the public schools. Therefore, the program has been carefully designed to avoid the threat of significantly defunding the public school system. In the case of the business rebate, the program limits the rebate to just 10 percent of a business' school tax bill. This means that even if every business in Chicago applied for an Education Rebate, and if every firm donated the maximum amount to *nonpublic* schools, the public schools would lose less than 2 percent of their current tax revenues.

Conclusion

The Education Rebate program creates a bottom line for the Chicago Public Schools by reducing the tax penalty on parents who withdraw their children from ineffective or undesired public schools. The absence of a bottom line was one three principal factors in the decline of the Chicago Public Schools described in Chapter Five.

Education Rebates are fair because they recognize that people who voluntarily contribute to a child's education should not have to pay again in taxes for a public school system that has failed to serve them well. Education Rebates are equitable because they extend the same choice to low-income and poor families that only the wealthy can now afford. Education Rebates are essential to education reform in Chicago because they produce healthy competition among public schools, and between public schools and nonpublic schools, for individual and corporate contributions as well as for students.

Because the Education Rebate plan includes nonpublic as well as public schools, it will be criticized by the many special interest groups that profit from the public school system's present uncompetitive environment. The reader should keep in mind, though, that nonpublic schools have historically played a major role providing mass education in the U.S., and continue to do so in Chicago today. If the primary purpose of education reform is to help our children learn, then solutions that go beyond the public schools cannot be dismissed out of hand. Helping all children, regardless of what schools they happen to attend, should be our objective.

Notes

1. David S. Seeley writes: "No matter how dissatisfied poor families may be, they are pretty much stuck with the public schools -- and usually the poorest public schools. For them, public education operates as a monopoly that has little need to satisfy its customers. Not only are educational services for poor families usually of poorer quality, but poor families' lack of choice tends to keep them that way." David S. Seeley, "The Choice-Equity Dilemma: A Partial Solution," *Equity and Choice*, Winter 1987, p. 57.

2. Landlords would express annual payments made by each renter as a percentage of total annual rental income for the building. This percentage, expressed as a decimal, would be multiplied by the building's education property tax bill for the previous tax year. In this way, each renter's share of total rent paid to the landlord becomes the basis for determining each renter's share of the tax liability.

11

TUITION REBATES: TEN QUESTIONS AND ANSWERS

If parents are given a choice, public school officials will lose the monopoly power they now hold over a captive audience. That monopoly power is greatest over the poor, but it extends to all who cannot afford to simultaneously pay taxes for the public schools and tuition at a private school.

Thomas Sowell
Education: Assumptions versus History

1. **How will low-income people benefit from this plan?**

Every school-age child in Chicago benefits from the Education Rebate plan because it creates a bottom line for the Chicago Public Schools. Because they will face the prospect of losing revenue and enrollment if they fail to satisfy parents, the public schools will have to listen to every parent, and will have to do their best to educate every child.

153

The Education Rebate plan also helps low-income people in particular by giving them the same choice that wealthy families now take for granted. The plan does this by relieving the financial burden on families that opt to enroll their children in nonpublic schools.

Middle- and upper-income white families have always had the means to withdraw their children from the public schools and enroll them in nonpublic schools. An Education Rebate can be expected to have little effect on their decisions. Low-income families have only recently gained access to nonpublic schools or formed their own. For these families, education rebates would make an enormous difference.

Some people contend that upper- and middle-income parents would be more likely than low-income parents to use the rebates to leave the public school system. Although the Education Rebate plan is carefully designed to benefit renters as well as home-owners, and although the plan's ceilings and floors should help to avoid this problem, emotions make it hard for people to accept the facts. Many people have observed the years of "white flight" from the city, and though the overwhelming majority of white students withdrawn from the city's schools were enrolled in *public* schools in the suburbs, nevertheless nonpublic schools remain the target of much blame and resentment.

People who are afraid of the effects choice might have on the Chicago Public Schools should be aware that the problems facing the inner city have changed since the 1960s. Today, black instutitions, including businesses, schools, and associations are emerging in the inner city. A major problem they face is the flight of black professionals and the black middle class to suburban communities, some undoubtedly to find better quality public schools. Dr. Joan Davis Ratteray, in a seminal study of black nonpublic schools in Chicago's inner city, wrote:

The black middle class is abandoning its roots, leaving black educational institutions and in some cases moving out of black neighborhoods. This pattern of "black flight" can be seen in the dwindling numbers of students from black middle-income families enrolled in Chicago's independent neighborhood schools. It is supported by statistics on increased enrollment of blacks in magnet schools and in predominantly white private schools. In fact, studies have indicated that total enrollment of white private schools would have been constant were it not for an influx of minority students, both nationally and in Chicago itself.[1]

Many of the thousands of poor and minority parents of Chicago care greatly about the quality of schooling their children receive. These parents are not passively accepting low-quality public education in their communities. Writes Ratteray:

> Parents from low-income neighborhoods are continually seeking independent schools to help their children survive the schooling process, often doing so under great financial hardship. While there are many influences that tend to hamper the growth of these institutions, the schools continue to thrive.[2]

Another study of black enrollment in nonpublic schools, this one conducted by researchers at Northwestern University, found that "private schools are emerging as a significant competitor to public education for black students. This trend is likely to continue to increase, particularly if the public schools do not provide opportunities for social mobility for black children."[3]

It is odd that, in the face of this evidence, some people still claim that programs offering choice would benefit whites and the well-to-do at the expense of blacks and the poor. Everything points to just the opposite result.

2. Who Should Qualify for Rebates?

Under the Education Rebate plan, *everyone* who finances the educational expenses of a child attending a registered public or nonpublic school in Chicago would qualify for a rebate. Because more than one person could contribute toward the educational expenses of each child, the total value of rebates issued on behalf of one child could exceed the $1,000 limit placed on each rebate.

This policy has a number of advantages: it is fair, since anyone -- not only parents -- who contributes toward the education of a child should not have to pay again through taxes. It also benefits the poor, since those who are better able to afford the tuition can pay tuition for a particular child or contribute to schools serving low-income communities.

Allowing a child's relatives and friends to claim the rebate also would recognize the extended family structures common in many poor neighborhoods, where uncles, aunts, and grandparents typically contribute toward children's educational expenses. If rebates are restricted only to parents, these avenues of support will be excluded from the program.

Allowing everyone to qualify for the rebates gives those without children a voice in deciding which schools their tax dollars will support, a voice that currently is denied them. This is particularly important in Chicago, because nearly 80 percent of the taxpayers in Chicago do not have children enrolled in public schools. Education rebates give these taxpayers a greater incentive to scrutinize both public and nonpublic schools, *and* they give the public schools an incentive to listen to their concerns and interests.

Allowing businesses to qualify for Education Rebates also encourages greater scrutiny of the public schools, and consequently greater accountability. Businesses have a very large stake in the success of the public schools because they must bear the costs of retraining people who leave the public schools unable to read, write, or perform basic arithmetic. "Many industries are already experiencing shortages of adequately trained workers and others fear that they will soon face this prospect," according to Leonard Lund, an educational specialist with the Conference Board, a nonprofit research group financed by business. According to a Conference Board survey of 130 major corporations, nearly two-thirds consider primary and secondary education their number one community affairs concern, up from less than half in 1985.[4] In addition, businesses pay half the property taxes that support the schools, so as a matter of equity they can claim a voice in the operation of the schools.

The business community has reacted positively when asked to comment on tax relief plans linked to aid for education. A survey of business attitudes conducted by Barry J. Carroll for the U.S. Department of Education in 1984 found that 74 percent of the executives who responded to the question commented favorably on a tax credit plan for corporate aid to education.[5]

Some parents and teachers are opposed to giving business representatives a voice in the operation of the public schools. The goals and interests of the business community, they say, are often at odds with those of parents and educators. Parents and educators know best what is in the interest of school children, the argument goes, because they are closest to the children and are informed about teaching skills.

The debate between advocates and critics of business involvement in the public schools would be settled quickly if parents, teachers, and businesspeople could choose to enroll their children in, or given financial support to, those schools that have the degree of business representation they feel is right. Some schools, for example, could reject corporate involvement completely; others could encourage maximum corporate involvement even in sensitive areas like curriculum and management.

The Education Rebate plan encourages greater business participation in the public schools as well as the nonpublic schools. But by limiting business contributions to 10 percent of their local education tax liability, the plan limits the leverage that businesses have when negotiating with public school administrators. The Education Rebate plan begins the process of allowing businesses to become more involved in schooling, but it does not necessarily assure that they will gain greater representation in all, or even any, of the public schools.

3. Would Education Rebates drastically reduce the tax funds available to public schools?

The answer is no. There are two reasons why this will not happen. First, the plan is designed to limit the amount of money that can be diverted from the public schools. Second, under the plan the public schools must lose funding *more slowly than they lose enrollment*, so they would have more money to spend on fewer students. In other words, the public schools actually get a financial benefit from the plan.[6]

The amount of money individuals and businesses could choose to divert from the public schools under this plan is only a small fraction of the total amount of funds available to the schools. The average homeowner in Chicago, for example, pays $348 a year in property taxes to the Board of Education, and the average renter approximately the same.[7]

If every parent who currently has a child enrolled in a nonpublic school in Chicago qualifies

158

for a rebate equal to the entire amount of education property taxes paid by an average homeowner, the Board of Education would lose $44 million, or about 2.4 percent of its total current receipts.[8] This amount is significant enough to make the public schools realize they must compete against other school systems, but it is hardly so large that cuts in waste and bureaucracy could not easily accommodate it.

If one child of every twenty now enrolled in the public schools transferred to a nonpublic school, and again assuming that each child's parents applied for and received a rebate equal to their entire school property tax liability, the loss in property tax revenues to the public schools would be $7.3 million, or less than half of 1 percent of the Board of Education's budget. If one child in ten left the public schools, $14.6 million would be transferred from the control of public schools to individual parents. This is still less than 1 percent of the Board's budget.

If every business in Chicago chose to donate the maximum allowable percentage of its property tax liability to a nonpublic school, the loss of funds to the school system would be just 1.4 percent of the current level.

The second reason the public schools will not be damaged by the Education Rebate plan is that the Board of Education *saves* money by no longer having to teach the children who transfer to other schools. The average amount the public schools would save is roughly equal to the number of students who would transfer to nonpublic schools multiplied by the amount currently spent on each student each year, which was approximately $4,000 in 1987.[9] Since the average *revenue* loss for each child who leaves the public schools will probably be less than $400, the public schools are left with *more money per student* to spend.

Once again, let us look at what would happen if 5 percent of all children now in the public schools transferred to nonpublic schools or other public

159

school systems. The public schools could lose $7.3 million in property tax revenues, but the public school cost of educating those children would have been $84 million ($4,000 x 21,000), or over ten times that much. So the public schools would actually *benefit* from the program by having approximately $77 million more to spend on the students who are still enrolled in its schools. If fully 10 percent of the students now enrolled in the Chicago Public Schools transferred to schools elsewhere, the local revenue loss would be $14.6 million, the cost deferred would be $168 million, and the net benefit to the public schools would total $153.4 million.

Further information about the financial impact of Education Rebates on the Chicago Public Schools can be found in an appendix to this book.

4.   Why a ceiling of $1,000 and a floor of $300?

The Education Rebate program would allow rebates equal to the amount actually spent on a child's tuition, the amount paid directly or indirectly in education property taxes, or $1,000, whichever is least. For persons who pay little or no property taxes either directly (on their homes) or indirectly (through their rent), a minimum rebate of $300 or actual educational expenses paid, whichever is less, is set.

The $1,000 ceiling is suggested for a number of reasons. First, $1,000 is in the midrange of tuition charged by small nonpublic schools in Chicago. This means a rebate of this amount will bring substantial relief to the majority of parents enrolling their children in nonpublic schools. Second, $1,000 is approximately one-fourth as much as the Chicago Public Schools spend each year on each student. It can hardly be argued that tax relief of this size could give nonpublic schools an unfair advantage over public schools, since the latter receive four times the subsidy.

Exactly where the relief ceiling is set may not be an important issue from a public policy perspective, since very few families in Chicago will qualify for large amounts of relief. It is important to keep in mind that the maximum rebate is the $1,000 ceiling, actual spending on educational expenses, *or actual school property taxes paid, whichever is less*.
A small number of homeowners and renters in Chicago pay as much as $1,000 in school property taxes.

The $300 minimum rebate was selected for a number of reasons, too. The lowest annual tuition Dr. Ratteray found in her study of nonpublic schools in Chicago was $270 at the Humboldt Christian School (on North Humboldt Boulevard). The school has sources of support other than tuition, including contributions from the community, profits from a thrift shop, and substantial volunteer support. An Education Rebate of $300, then, would reimburse a parent for the entire tuition at an exceptional school such as Humboldt Christian.

Another reason for selecting the $300 figure is that it is below the estimated average rebate for which a homeowner could qualify ($348). This is important, since the underlying rationale for the program -- that people are taking back taxes they paid for a service they chose to fund voluntarily-- tells us that people collecting rebates larger than their direct or indirect tax liability should be the exception, not the rule.

5. When would the plan be implemented?

Legislation authorizing an Education Rebate plan could be passed in 1989, and the plan could be implemented sometime in 1990. To assure an orderly transition to the new system, the plan could be implemented in steps over a period of two or three years.

A tax credit proposal being circulated as a referendum question in California starts with a maximum credit of $100 per student and increases $100 a year until it reaches 25 percent of the average annual cost per student in public schools. A similar approach for Chicago might be to establish a $300 floor *and ceiling* immediately and gradually raise the ceiling to $1,000 over a three- or four-year period.

The Education Rebate plan could be implemented in a limited number of subdistricts at first, and then adopted in other subdistricts after a trial period. Advisory referenda could be used to determine the order in which districts would adopt the plan. A danger with this technique, however, is that it may diminish parental support and interest in the program. Many public school administrators, on the other hand, will be active and united in their opposition to the program. To mobilize parental support for the plan and to overcome the natural organizational advantages that these public employees have, it may be best to adopt the entire program at once.

6. Are Education Rebates constitutional?

Yes. The Supreme Court has ruled that parents, not the state, have ultimate authority in determining which school a child attends. In *Pierce v. Society of Sisters* (1925), the Court held that "[t]he child is not the mere creature of the state; those who nurture him and direct his destiny have the right, coupled with the high duty, to recognize and prepare him for additional obligations."[10] In reaching this conclusion, the Court explicitly rejected the notion that public schools should hold a legal monopoly on the education of our children.

In a more recent decision, (*Meuller v. Allen*, 1984), the Court dealt with the question of whether programs aimed at relieving the tax burden of parents with children in nonpublic schools could be constitutional. The Justices ruled that such programs *are* constitutional so long as they defray school expenses at *both public and nonpublic schools*; the tax mechanisms used have multiple purposes and effects, not primarily the effect of inhibiting or advancing religion; and government funding (or tax relief) goes to the parents rather than directly to schools.[11]

It is clear that the Renters and Homeowners Education Rebate program passes this Constitutional test easily. Persons who contribute to the educational expenses of any child enrolled in a Chicago school -- whether public or nonpublic -- would qualify for an Education Rebate. The property tax that is used as the tax mechanism for providing relief finances a broad range of services and has many other exclusions (such as the Homestead exemption) for publicly desirable goals. And no government funds are being given to any nonpublic school under this plan; only parents are receiving checks from the County Treasurer, and even then the checks are only a *rebate* of taxes previously paid (except for low-income people qualifying for the relief floor).

The Supreme Court has also ruled on which educational expenses may be reimbursed. This can be a difficult question, because some expenses at some religiously oriented schools may be seen as supporting the views of a particular religious sect. The Education Rebate plan carefully accommodates this difficulty by using the same description of qualifying expenses as is used in the Supreme Court-approved Minnesota education tax deduction law. That law reads, in part:

> the amount paid to others . . . for tuition, textbooks, and transportation of each dependent in attending an elementary or secondary school . . . wherein a resident of this state may legally fulfill the state's compulsory attendance laws, which is not operated for profit, and which adheres to

the provisions of the Civil Rights Act of 1964 and Chapter 363. As used in this clause, "textbooks" includes books and other instructional materials and equipment used in elementary and secondary schools in teaching only those subjects legally and commonly taught in public elementary and secondary schools in this state. "Textbooks" does not include instructional books and materials used in the teaching of religious tenets, doctrines, or worship, the purpose of which is to instill such tenets, doctrines, or worship, nor does it include books or materials for, or transportation to, extracurricular activities including sporting events, musical or dramatic events, speech activities, driver's education, or similar programs.[12]

7. **How would this plan affect desegregation efforts in Chicago?**

The Education Rebate plan could be expected to encourage a degree of voluntary integration significantly beyond that which currently exists in Chicago. It would do this by giving greater choice to families who are now required to send their children to geographically assigned, racially segregated neighborhood schools.

Many of Chicago's public schools are now racially segregated. In 1983, nineteen high schools had enrollments that were entirely minority students, and another seventeen were at least 90 percent minority. Only nineteen schools were classified by Designs for Change as integrated.[13] Major reasons for this pattern of segregation are the high percentage of the student population that is now minority (approximately 85 percent) and the racial concentration of neighborhoods in Chicago.

The Education Rebate plan would encourage racial integration in two ways. First, it would lower the financial barrier now facing low-income minority families wishing to enroll their children in nonpublic schools. Some of these schools have substantial nonminority enrollments drawn from upper-income, typically white, families. Second, allowing choice within the public school system will lead parents to enroll their children in schools that offer the best curriculum or learning environment for their children. These schools are less likely to be racially segregated than is the geographically assigned school to which parents currently must send their children. Other cities have found that parents are willing to overlook race when choosing a public school for their children; a choice program in Memphis, for example, led to "greatly enhanced voluntary desegregation."[14]

8. Would expenses paid to any school in Chicago qualify a parent for rebates?

When designing a program, it is necessary that we anticipate the actions of persons who would abuse the program for their personal gain or for other noneducational purposes. For example, what if a notorious street gang or group of terrorists started a "school" for children, and the parents of children enrolled in the "school" applied for Education Rebates? Would the parents' application be approved by the County Treasurer? Similarly, could sham schools be established for the purpose of issuing fake receipts to parents who could then apply for Education Rebates? These are serious threats that need to be addressed.

Luckily, the Illinois State Board of Education already has *registration* and *recognition* procedures that allow us to distinguish between genuine nonpublic schools and fakes or shams.[15] By reimbursing only those educational expenses incurred by enrollment of a child in a registered or recognized school, the pretenders can be denied funding under the plan.

The Illinois State Board of Education has established policies and guidelines, developed with the assistance of nonpublic school personnel, to determine if nonpublic schools are in compliance with federal and state laws regarding health examination and immunization, attendance, number of hours of instruction, nondiscrimination, and fire and health safety requirements. The state requires all nonpublic elementary and secondary schools in Illinois to *register* with the state and submit a report to the state each year showing that they have met these minimum requirements. Entities that fail to register may not operate as schools, and the children enrolled in them are considered truants.

In addition to registration, the state also has a voluntary *recognition* procedure, part of which is regular inspection of the school by the staff of the Nonpublic School Approval Section of the Illinois State Board of Education. Schools may gain state recognition by complying with a range of governance, curriculum, facility, and personnel requirements set by the State. These requirements are more rigorous than the requirements for registration, and some schools choose not to pursue this designation.

Under the Education Rebate plan, only education expenses associated with a child's enrollment at a *registered* or *recognized* school would qualify for reimbursement by the County Treasurer. Legislation implementing the Education Rebate program will define the term "nonpublic school" as any entity that satisfies the state Board of Education's registration and recognition guidelines in effect on January 1, 1988. Any revision of those guidelines that would make them more restrictive would be of no force or effect for the purposes of the Education Rebate plan. Tuition or other expenses paid on behalf of a student attending a school that is not registered with or recognized by the State Board of Education would not qualify a parent for a rebate, regardless of the amount spent or the amount of school property taxes paid. This policy should be sufficient to prevent abuse of the plan without being so restrictive that creative alternative schools would be disqualified.

9. How does this plan differ from "voucher" plans?

A voucher plan for education would have a government agency issue "vouchers" or certificates redeemable for a certain level of educational services by any public or nonpublic school. Nobel Prize-winning economist Milton Friedman, father of the idea, described it like this:

> Governments could require a minimum level of schooling financed by giving parents vouchers redeemable for a specified maximum sum per child per year if spent on "approved" educational services. Parents would then be free to spend this sum and any additional sum they themselves provided on purchasing educational services from an "approved" institution of their own choice. The educational services could be rendered by private enterprises operated for profit, or by non-profit institutions.[16]

Battles have been fought for over twenty years to implement educational vouchers in the United States, including a number of bills introduced here in Illinois. Strong support for voucher plans exists in many circles.[17] Opposition to voucher plans is fierce among public school teachers and administrators, and their lobbying efforts have been largely successful in preventing implementation of such plans. A few federal experiments with tuition vouchers occurred during the 1970s, and the state of Vermont has a program of very long standing that is similar in many respects to a voucher plan, but other attempts to implement voucher plans at the national and state levels have been frustrated.[18]

The Education Rebate program differs conceptually from voucher plans in four ways. First, the amount of government aid is largely determined by the participant's direct or indirect tax liability (except for subsidized rebates to the poor), not by the amount being spent on tuition or educational expenses. This means the Education Rebate program asks only that parents *get back* their tax dollars for state-provided educational services they are not using or have supported voluntarily. Voucher plans ask that the government grant be some predetermined amount or be determined by how much the family is spending on education, even if this amount is more than what the family paid in education taxes.[19]

The second difference is that a voucher plan gives government agencies greater potential control over the institutions that qualify for the vouchers. A rebate plan relies on the same reporting procedures as are used by persons seeking tax deductions for charitable giving. It is the applicant, not the school, that may be called for an audit and asked to produce proof of the legitimacy of his claim. Voucher plans, on the contrary, require that the schools deal directly with the government to redeem the certificates, and could compel schools to comply with whatever procedures and requirements the government establishes. While some fear that government agencies will use their power to discriminate against some nonpublic schools,[20] others fear the misguided benevolence of government regulators even more.[21]

The third major difference between rebates and vouchers is that participants in a rebate program must *first* make their expenditures on education and only then apply for tax relief. This means that people are not being implicitly instructed by the program to "shop around" for a new school for their child, but are only being told that the financial penalty of doing so will be relieved after the fact.

Only those parents who *do* choose to make independent expenditures are made part of the program. There is no mass mailing of certificates and a sudden need for parents to make a choice; people can choose to enter the program or not.

The fourth difference between the two programs is that rebates give public schools a stronger position from which to compete against nonpublic schools. Under some voucher plans, public and nonpublic schools would compete on equal footing for the certificates, and the value of the certificates would be expected to amount to the bulk of the schools' entire budgets. But presumably public schools would still operate under mandates of open enrollment (within their local recruitment area or district), special services to the handicapped, uniform curriculum, and the many state and federal regulations. Many public school administrators fear that this is unequal competition and an invitation to "cream skimming" by their nonpublic competitors.

The rebate plan exposes the public schools to much less risk. It threatens to reduce the tax funds going to the public schools by a relatively small amount, and does not alter existing commitments for state and federal aid to the public schools. In fact, the plan's recommendation that the state general aid formula be modified to continue per-pupil payments for one or two years after a child leaves a school allows the state to compensate schools for part of whatever losses might occur to local property tax funding.

The point of this discussion is to suggest that voucher plans are different from, not necessarily inferior to, a rebate plan. There may be many advantages of voucher plans that the rebate plan does not capture. But the Education Rebate plan presented here offers a better chance of winning approval by voters in Chicago, and of accommodating the real concerns of people in both the public schools and the nonpublic schools here in Chicago. No voucher plan has ever been proposed that would be specific to Chicago and that would not immediately endanger the public school system. These strategic concerns are important now, as passage of school reform legislation appears imminent.

10. Have education rebates been tried anywhere else?

No, but programs similar to it are rapidly gaining ground across the country. Programs that would allow parental choice among *public* schools have been endorsed by a long list of prestigious national organizations, including the National Governors' Association, the Committee for Economic Development, the Carnegie Task Force on Teaching as a Profession, and the National PTA.[22] Extending choice to nonpublic schools, however, has been more controversial.

Tax *deductions* for educational expenses are allowed by law in Minnesota and Iowa. Minnesota allows a deduction of up to $1,000 for educational expenses. Tuition tax deduction laws are pending in two other states, Massachusetts and California.

A *voucher-like* plan for education exists in Vermont, where public school districts are allowed to pay for the tuition of children enrolled in nonpublic schools. Though no certificates actually change hands, the program has many of the characteristics of a voucher plan. It operates in school districts having 25 percent of the state's population.[23]

Finally, a tax *credit* plan for education is being circulated as a referendum question by a group of parents in California. That program would be the first such plan implemented in the U.S.

170

Notes

1. Joan Davis Ratteray, "Access to Quality: Private Schools in Chicago's Inner City" (Chicago: The Heartland Institute, June 27, 1986), p. 8.
2. Ibid.
3. Diana T. Slaughter and Barbara L. Schneider, *Newcomers: Blacks in Private Schools*, Final Report to the National Institute of Education, February, 1986, p. 593.
4. Associated Press, "Education is top concern of business," *Chicago Sun-Times*, January 12, 1987.
5. Barry J. Carroll, *Talking With Business*, U.S. Department of Education, 1984, p. 29.
6. For additional information on this question, as well as commentary on the effects of Education Rebates on state aid to the Chicago Public Schools, see the appendix titled "The Financial Impact of Education Rebates."
7. This estimate is based on tax rates in effect in 1987 on a home with a market value of $40,000, approximately the average market value of a home in Chicago in 1986. This estimate was produced by Richard Van Ecko, Cook County Assessors Office, and is based on 1986 overall assessment figures and overall parcel count for Class 2 properties. Because Class 2 includes garages and small apartment buildings, an attempt was made to correct the figure by averaging. The 1986 assessed values were based on reassessments done in 1982, 1983, 1984, and 1985. There was no general reassessment made in any part of the city in 1986.
8. Enrollment in Chicago nonpublic schools totalled 126,000 in 1986-87. Illinois State Board of Education, *Nonpublic Registration, Enrollment, and Staff Report, 1986-87 (Springfield, 1987)*.
9. Actually, the amount saved would be equal to the number of students who transfer times the *marginal* cost of educating each of those child-

ren. The marginal cost (or the cost of the "last" student added to enrollment) may be more or less than the average cost, depending on each school's situation. It is not clear that, for the system as a whole, marginal cost would tend to be more or less than average cost; for that reason, average cost is used as an approximation of the systemwide savings.

10. See *Whose Child is This?* by the Illinois Advisory Committee on Nonpublic Schools, 1978, for a thorough discussion of parental authority in education.

11. For a discussion of earlier Court decisions, see "Educational Tax Credits," by Roger A. Freeman, in *The Public School Monopoly*, edited by Robert B. Everhardt, (San Francisco: Pacific Institute for Public Policy Research, 1982), pp. 471-502; and the Catholic League for Religious and Civil Rights, *How to Debate Tuition Tax Credits* (Milwaukee, Wisconsin, 1983), pp. 1-13.

12. Minnesota Code, Chapter 268, Article 1, Section 13.

13. Designs for Change, *The Bottom Line* (Chicago, January 1985), p. 109.

14. Steven A. Wolfgram, "Education by Choice," April 1987, p. 13. Also see Janet R. Price and Jane R. Stern, "Magnet Schools as a Strategy for Integration and School Reform," *Yale Law and Policy Review*, Vol. 5, No. 2, Spring/ Summer 1987.

15. Illinois State Board of Education, *Policy and Guidelines for Registration and Recognition of Nonpublic Elementary and Secondary Schools*, March 1984.

16. Milton Friedman, *Capitalism and Freedom*, (Chicago: The University of Chicago Press, 1962), p. 89.

17. See, for example: Thomas Sowell, *Education: Assumptions vs. History* (Stanford, CA: Hoover Institution Press, 1986), pp. 103-106; E.G. West, "The Prospects for Educational Vouchers: An Economic Analysis," in Everhardt, pp. 369-392;

and Virgil C. Blum, *Education: Freedom and Competition* (Chicago: Argus Communications Co., 1967).

18. See John McClaughry, "Who Says Vouchers Wouldn't Work?" *Reason*, January 1984, and *Educational Choice in Vermont* (Concord, VT: Institute for Liberty and Community, 1987).

19. In the final analysis, a refundable rebate program could be functionally equivalent to a voucher plan with participants eligible only for low dollar amounts. But the rationale for the rebate is sufficiently different from that of the voucher to assure that the eligibility requirements, floors, and ceilings would be set at different levels. Under the rebate program, parents qualify for aid by the act of reducing the state's financial obligation, not by paying tuition at a private school. This distinction may also have constitutional implications: see Roger A. Freeman, p. 483.

20. See Dwight R. Lee, "The Political Economy of Educational Vouchers," *The Freeman*, July 1986.

21. Denis Doyle, for example, says "I must confess that were enactment likely I would be nervous indeed, because the predilection of congress and state legislatures would be to smother private schools with affection." In "The Role of the School in a Post-Industrial Democracy," a commissioned paper prepared for Dingle Associates, Inc. under the terms of a NIE contract, January 1983, p. 19.

22. William Snider, "The Call for Choice," *Education Week*, June 24, 1987.

23. John McClaughry, *Educational Choice in Vermont*.

12

OTHER REFORM PROPOSALS

> *Major restructuring of the system must emphasize return of school governance to parents and community, return of authority to the principal, and recognition of the paramount importance of the teacher and support of the teacher's work.*
>
> Chicago Partnership
> *Position on Education Reform in Chicago*

Many people have devoted countless hours of their time to trying to improve the Chicago Public Schools. Some of these people have sought to change the schools "from the inside," working for incremental improvements within the current organization. Others have worked from outside the system, proposing reforms based on their research or personal experiences. The dialogue and original research produced by all these people have been indispensable to the education reform movement in Chicago.

In this chapter we discuss three of the many plans being debated at the time this book was prepared. These plans are being put forward by very influential groups, and they represent some of the best thinking on education reform available today. Each plan contains provisions that would benefit public education in Chicago, and we urge readers to talk with the people who are promoting these proposals.

The authors of this book believe that these plans, though they make valuable contributions to the debate, are inadequate to the task we face. We present here fair descriptions of the plans and our reservations about them.

Chicago Teachers Union Proposal

The Chicago Teachers Union (CTU) has put forward a reform plan, titled "Revitalizing the Chicago Public Schools in 1988," that contains sixteen major recommendations.[1] These recommendations address five key areas:

School-based management. Give existing local school improvement councils greater authority over the nonpersonnel budget, local school policies, and curriculum objectives, as well as the power to select the principal. Authority to select staff, adopt programs, and develop curriculum would be held by a School Management Team composed of the principal, delegates from local school unions, three community representatives, and a majority of classroom teachers.

Teacher professionalism. Create internship, peer assistance, and peer intervention programs to support recruitment and professional development of teachers. Provide higher pay for teachers and salary incentives for classroom instruction.

Reduce class size. Hire more teachers and make better use of existing personnel and facilities to reduce average class size.

Improve staff and teacher training. Develop and implement a "systemwide staff development program" and adopt the teacher training techniques developed by the American Federation of Teachers (the CTU's parent union).

Eliminate unnecessary paperwork. Paperwork "steals valuable time" from teachers pursuing their true objective -- educating children. It must be reduced.

The teachers who work in the Chicago Public Schools are uniquely qualified to put forward plans concerning teacher training and support programs. Such programs as are described in recommendations Two and Four above, by influencing the quality of instruction, could improve student performance and are worth pursuing. Similarly, recommendation Five will find few critics, since freeing teachers of the burden of unnecessary paperwork is an admirable goal.

The union's call for higher teacher salaries and smaller class sizes flies in the face of evidence, presented in Chapter Seven, that teacher salaries and total spending on education are not significantly associated with improved student performance. Moreover, in Chapter One we explained that public school teachers in Illinois are already the tenth highest paid in the country, and average annual teacher salaries in Chicago are some $5,000 more than in the rest of the state. Chicago has already tried higher teacher salaries; they have not secured better education for our students.

The CTU's plan for school-based management is a movement in the correct direction, since more authority held by school-based personnel will give parents and the community greater access to decision makers. But this plan would place the most important forms of authority -- over budget, curriculum, and personnel matters -- in the hands of a School Management Team dominated by teachers, the principal, and union representatives, not parents or community representatives. This is unlikely to produce the degree of accountability or responsiveness necessary for effective schools to emerge. Moreover, it is unlikely that parents and community members will long participate in a process where once again real authority and input are withheld.

Conspicuously absent from the CTU proposal are any provisions for choice or competition among schools. The CTU plan would leave in place the practice of geographic assignment of children to schools, meaning parents may not choose better schools for their children. Parents who seek better schools outside the Chicago Public Schools would still be punished for their choice by having to pay both school taxes and private school tuition. Because it does not allow competition among schools, the CTU plan would fail to solve the problems of curriculum selection, bureaucratic growth, and unaccountability documented in earlier chapters. For these reasons we believe it is inadequate.

Mayor's Education Summit Proposal

In 1986, the late Mayor Harold Washington called together business leaders and school administrators in an attempt to start a partnership for improving the Chicago Public Schools. After the 1987 teachers' strike, the group was expanded to include parents and teachers. In April 1988, the group, operating under the title of the Mayor's Education Summit, released a series of reform proposals.[2] Highlights of this reform package are:

Strengthen the school-based management team. Establish training, networking, and mentoring programs for administrators, teachers, and principals.

178

Give the principal greater responsibility over his or her school, and greater authority over personnel and budgetary matters. (37 recommendations)

Encourage parent/community outreach. Provide training for parents interested in participating in Local School Bodies (LSBs), composed of the principal, two teachers, two community representatives, and six parents. Give LSBs authority to select principals (with review by General Superintendent); approve or disapprove textbook expenditures; "supplement the required core curriculum . . . to meet the unique needs of the school"; and review, amend, and approve a lump sum budget prepared by the principal within systemwide guidelines. (28 recommendations)

Streamline the central office. The central office would retain wide powers, including: collective bargaining and labor relations, strategic planning, "establish equitable systemwide policy and standards in appropriate areas (such as core curriculum, performance standards, testing and assessment, principal performance contracts, employee evaluation, due process, security, safety, facilities, financial management . . .)," training and technical assistance for administrators, systemwide personnel policy and operations, and "to ensure that funds are spent in the most cost effective manner by implementing processes and procedures throughout the system that emphasize the efficient utilization of limited resources to maximize quality education." (7 recommendations)

Improve student performance. Establish systemwide goals for reduction in dropout rate, improvement in daily attendance rates, and improved test scores; pledge that "school staff will have high expectations and respect for every student"; impose a core curriculum of approved materials screened "to assure fairness in relation to race, ethnicity, gender and income status"; develop partnerships with businesses

179

for support, training, and employment assistance; increase funding to reduce class size and increase the number of support personnel; and improve communication between the school and parents. (63 recommendations)

Professionalize Teaching. Establish internship, peer assistance, local staff development, and mentor programs; increase teacher salaries; authorize school incentive grants for improved schools; lengthen school day; aggressively recruit new teachers; require an academic major along with education courses for new teachers; utilize experts from business, but require provisional certification of persons engaging in extended classroom teaching. (38 recommendations)

The Mayor's Education Summit proposal clearly shows a familiarity with some of the effective schools literature described in Chapter Seven. It gives the principal greater authority and responsibility over the operation of schools and creates a larger role for parents and other community members through the Local School Bodies. The proposal's call for greater communication with parents and the business community is commendable, as are its suggestions (similar to those of the Chicago Teachers Union) for professional development programs for teachers.

Missing from the Summit proposal are provisions specifically aimed at reducing the school system's massive bureaucracy. The central office under this plan would retain enormous powers and responsibilities, and perhaps would have even greater control over curriculum. Many of the responsibilities listed for the central board read like invitations to retain or even expand its involvement in the day-to-day operation of the schools. It is hard to imagine that individual school autonomy, seemingly promised by the new powers given to principals and LSBs, could be realized with a central office so deeply involved in the same areas.

Also missing from the Summit proposal is a call for choice or competition. Like the Chicago Teachers Union plan, this plan would leave in place the practice of geographic assignment of students to schools, along with the tax penalty on parents who remove their children from the system. Without this competitive element, the many statements of goals and objectives ring hollow. Why should parents or businesses participate in partnerships with the schools if they are still a captive audience? How can a simple proclamation that "staff will have high expectations" have any effect whatsoever so long as the staff is protected from the bottom line?

The Summit proposal is a complex document that was still undergoing revision at the time this book was written. But we believe it misses the target of fundamental restructuring of the school by a wide mark. By refusing to consider seriously a reduction in the power and size of the central office, and by ignoring the mounting call for choice and competition, the Summit has failed to produce a blueprint for genuine reform.

Chicago Partnership Proposal

The Chicago Partnership is a coalition of eight leading civic and advocacy organizations in Chicago. Chicago United, Inc., a member of the Partnership, has been asked to develop and promote a proposal that all group members could endorse. In March 1988 the Partnership released a position paper on education reform, and in April it led a group of thirteen other organizations in putting forward amendments to the Education Summit Proposal.[3] The Partnership's proposal is not a detailed plan, nor does it contain (as does the Education Summit proposal) a list of recommendations. Instead, the proposal puts forward the following seven "performance indicators":

181

Strengthen school-site management. Use elections to select members to the local school improvement councils (LSICs); give LSICs authority to hire, appraise, and dismiss principals; allow LSICs to review, approve, and audit school plans created by principals; give principals "full authority to allocate all available resources and to give direction to the school program, academic and otherwise."

Reduce significantly the size of the central administration. Move decision making and accountability to the school level; reduce central office staff through attrition, retirement, early retirement, and voluntary separation programs; contract out for goods, maintenance, and support services now provided or performed by school board employees; central office retains oversight and coordination powers in areas of tax levies, capital needs, labor relations, court-ordered programs, personnel policies, etc.

Encourage student and parental choice. "In order to foster competition, we propose choice of school for parents and students, intra-district and inter-district"; provide additional resources "for schools in need for the purpose of training and technical assistance."

Set goals for educational outcomes. Adopt as systemwide goals achievement of national norms on test scores in five years and on dropout rates in ten years.

Professionalize teachers, principals, and administrators. Enact many of the same programs advocated by the Chicago Teachers Union and Education Summit, including mentoring, peer consultation, etc; adopt merit pay; train principals for administrative responsibilities; begin a Principals' Academy independent of the school system.

Train parents and community representatives for school site governance. "We believe the best method of providing such training is through private sources. . . . The business community will assist in raising the funds needed to provide the service."

Transfer education research to classrooms. Establish partnerships between the Board of Education and local colleges, create Principals' Academy, teacher training institutes, etc.

The Chicago Partnership proposal is a dramatic improvement over the CTU and Education Summit plans. Like the Education Summit, it calls for strong community representation on a newly empowered local school improvement council, but it goes on to ensure that this transfer of power is real by recommending a reduction in the size and authority of the central authority. Moreover, it gives the principal all of the powers of a chief executive officer, and structures his relationship to the LSIC as that of a CEO to his board of directors.

The Partnership plan also calls for choice within the public school system, a necessary element of structural reform that we have emphasized throughout this book. The Partnership observes that "excellence thrives in an atmosphere and environment of competition," and "where there is competition there is reward, recognition and further opportunity. The system will renew itself and improve itself dynamically."[4] The Partnership does not describe a choice plan, saying instead that it will "work with organizations that propose experiments that foster competition in an academically appropriate manner." No mention is made of the tax penalty on parents with children enrolled in private schools.

The Partnership's calls for setting performance goals for the school system and professionalizing teachers and principals are similar to those made by the Education Summit, and are useful components of reform. Its advocacy of private sector training for local school improvement council members is also appropriate.

Conclusion

The Chicago Teachers Union plan for school reform points in the correct direction, but fails to prescribe badly needed restructuring of the Chicago Public Schools. The Mayor's Education Summit plan is worthy of praise because it gives parents and community members greater representation and authority in local school improvement councils, but it fails to attack the central problems of centralization, bureaucracy, and the absence of choice. The Chicago Partnership proposal is an excellent summary of necessary components of true reform, but is not actually a plan for implementing these components.

We hope the proponents of these reform proposals will see ways to accomplish their goals in either the C.U.R.E. or Education Rebate plans. We look forward to working with everyone -- educators, administrators, parents, and business representatives -- to produce the best possible cure for Chicago's public school crisis.

Notes

1. Chicago Teachers Union, *Perspective II: Re-vitalizing the Chicago Public Schools in 1988*, February 1988; "Chicago Teachers Union Urges Teacher-Parent Partnership," press release dated February 9, 1988, CTU; and *Fitting it all Together: School-Based Management in Chicago*, undated, CTU.
2. Mayor's Education Summit on Education Reform, *Preliminary Recommendations*, adopted March 21, 1988.
3. Chicago United, Inc., *The Chicago Partnership Position on Educational Reform in Chicago*, March 1988; and *Proposed Amendments to Mayor's Education Summit Proposals to Reform Public Education*, April 6, 1988.
4. Chicago United, Inc., *The Chicago Partnership Position*, p. 5.

13

WHAT YOU CAN DO

> *Just as the opportunities for genuine and lasting reform have never been greater, so too have the dangers of failure never been more stark. The future belongs to the educated. It remains to be seen whether Americans will seize the moment for education reform.*
>
> Denis P. Doyle and
> Terry W. Hartle
> *Excellence in Education:*
> *The States Take Charge*

This book presents a clear and forceful description of the education crisis facing Chicago. We have discussed dropout rates, test scores, spending levels, and parental participation. We have searched for the underlying structural causes of the problems that afflict the Chicago Public Schools, and we have found three interwoven factors: barriers to parental involvement, bureaucracy, and lack of accountability. We have put forward reforms that are practical and promise to be effective.

187

The children who enroll in the first grade in Chicago's public schools this Fall will graduate in the year 2000. How good will their education be during these twelve years? We believe adoption of either of the two reform proposals put forward in this book will have dramatic affects on their schools, their learning, and their lives.

Education in the Year 2000

In the year 2000, Chicago will have a public school system that is the envy of the nation. A higher proportion of students enrolled in Chicago high schools will graduate than students enrolled in high schools in the rest of the nation. They will graduate with higher reading scores and superior mathematical ability. They will have been exposed to values, courses, and teaching methods that their parents helped select. And they will be sought after eagerly by employers across the country and even around the world. A high school diploma from the Chicago Public Schools will be a source of pride and a ticket to higher education or employment security.

Those who work in the schools will be held in high esteem in their communities and by educators across the country. Teachers and principals will spend less time battling bureaucracy and filling out forms, and more time with students and parents. Funds no longer wasted on unproductive administrators or ineffective programs will be diverted to teacher pay and to the real needs of the schools. Excellence will be rewarded, innovation encouraged, and accountability assured. Teacher morale will be high because management will be more responsive to teachers' needs and opinions.

Education outside the public schools also will flourish. If the Education Rebate program were adopted, many nonpublic schools would operate side-by-side with the public schools, offering curricula

188

carefully adapted to the interests of parents and the needs of students. Catholic schools, as well as other religious and nonreligious schools, would open their doors even further to the low-income and disadvantaged, bringing unique prescriptions of "what works" to every child and parent who didn't find satisfaction in the public schools.

It is popular, in this age of skepticism, to make fun of optimism and hope. But what we are describing here is no mere dream or vision. It is the result of clear thinking about, and careful planning for, our most important social institution: education. What is missing is not a plan or the means for action; what is missing is the will to act.

What you can do

We must act, and act quickly, for reform to become a reality in Chicago. Here is what you can do:

1. Write and call your state legislator, city alderman, and school board members.

Letters to elected and appointed officials *do* get read, and they can have an enormous influence on the legislative process. If you do not know who your elected representatives are, call your local public library or board of elections.

When you contact these officials, tell them you are aware of the shortcomings of the public schools, and you are convinced of the need for true restructuring of the school system. Tell them you support proposals containing the voice and choice components of the C.U.R.E. and/or Education Rebate plans. Ask them to examine these proposals seriously and support them when the issues come before them in meetings or for votes.

189

2.   Learn the details of the C.U.R.E. plan.

For a copy of the complete legislative proposal containing the C.U.R.E. plan for parental choice and decentralization of the Chicago Public Schools, contact:

Chicagoans United to Reform Education
220 South State Street, Suite 1900
Chicago, Illinois 60604
312/922-0317

Please send $5 to cover the cost of printing and shipping this document.

3.   Buy multiple copies of this book for your friends and neighbors.

This is the only book that summarizes current research on the Chicago Public Schools and presents the reform proposals most likely to correct their problems. Most people will read a book if someone they know recommends it or gives it to them as a gift. Please consider buying extra copies to give to your friends and neighbors, so they too will be motivated to act on behalf of our children.

An order form for purchasing copies of this book at quantity discounts appears on the last page of this book. If the form already has been taken, contact:

URF Education Foundation
320 North Michigan Avenue, Suite 23N-B
Chicago, Illinois 60601
312/558-9080

4. **Support those organizations that are fighting for real educational reform in Chicago.**

The organizations that cosponsored production of this book are supported by individual, corporate, and foundation contributions. They rely on voluntary aid from people like you to continue their work. They can be contacted at these addresses:

United Republican Fund of Illinois
320 North Michigan Avenue, Suite 23N
Chicago, Illinois 60601
312/558-9080

URF Education Foundation
320 North Michigan Avenue, Suite 23N-B
Chicago, Illinois 60601
312/558-9080

The Heartland Institute
59 East Van Buren Street, Suite 810
Chicago, Illinois 60605
312/427-3060

Illinois Council on Democratic Policy
300 West Adams Street, Suite 610
Chicago, Illinois 60606
312/606-0690

A Parting Thought

For many years it has been fashionable to criticize Chicago's public schools but to do little to improve them. Now we have a genuine opportunity to reform them. The authors and sponsors of this book have made major donations of their time, energies, and money to getting this message out to a large audience.

The rest is up to you. Please write or call your public leaders today.

APPENDIX:

The Financial Impact of Education Rebates

The following data are used in estimating the financial impact of Education Rebates on the Chicago Public Schools:

Enrollment
  Public Schools: 420,000
  Nonpublic Schools: 126,000

Chicago Board of Education Budget
  1985 property tax levy: $ 507 million
  1987 All Fund Budget: 1,800 million
  1987 General Fund Budget: 1,700 million

Public School spending per pupil: $4,000

1985 education property taxes
paid by business: $ 250 million

Average education property tax
liability for a homeowner: $ 348

State aid per pupil in Chicago
Public Schools: $2,057

Lost Property Tax Revenues to the
Chicago Board of Education

A. The Absolute Maximum Possible Diversion

The amount of tax revenues that could be diverted from the Chicago Board of Education to the families of children enrolled in nonpublic schools, or specially earmarked to benefit students in particular public schools, depends on the level of public participation in the program. We believe that some, but certainly not all, parents will apply for the rebates. Many who apply will have made qualifying school expenditures insufficient to cancel out completely their direct or indirect property tax liabilities. Many contributions will go to individual *public* schools, so the money will return to the public school system but will not pass through the central administrative offices.

The maximum possible revenue diversion from the public school system would occur if every renter, homeowner, and business in Chicago chose to make qualifying contributions to or pay expenses at nonpublic schools; if every renter, homeowner, and business actually applied for a rebate; if every rebate awarded were for the total education property tax liability of the applicant; and if none of the contributions were made to a public school. No objective commentator would contend that these assumptions are realistic, but these assumptions do allow us to mark the *absolute maximum* amount of tax funds that could leave the public school system.

In this scenario, the Board of Education would lose *all* property tax revenues from homeowners and renters (approximately $250 million) and 10 percent of tax revenues from businesses (approximately $25 million). Total revenues lost would be $275 million. This is 15 percent of the Chicago Board of Education's total budget. It is not inconceivable that a restructured and more efficient Board of Education could sustain a revenue loss of this size, but once again this scenario is not even remotely possible.

B. More Realistic Scenarios

Participation rates: Three features of the Education Rebate plan tend to reduce the participation rate among parents who are not truly dissatisfied with their local public school. These factors are: educational expenses must be made before the rebate is applied for or awarded; a rebate will never exceed actual qualifying educational expenses; and participants must take the time to obtain information about qualifying schools before making their decision. These factors mean that participating in the program is not without a cost, and will not be worthwhile for people who are satisfied with their local public school or with the Chicago Public Schools generally.

The highest rates of participation in the program can be expected for those parents who already have children enrolled in nonpublic schools. While even for this group it would be unrealistic to project a 100 percent participation rate, we will use this projection in the scenarios below. The parents or guardians of school-age children attending public schools can be expected to have the next highest rate of participation, since some already are making educational expenditures that would be rebatable, while others will begin once the program becomes known. Because of the implicit costs of participating in the program, it seems unlikely that large numbers of nonparents would participate at first in the program.

In the scenarios below, we project that for every student currently enrolled in a nonpublic school, or transferred from a public school to a nonpublic school, one taxpayer will qualify for a rebate equal to the entire tax liability of the average homeowner. In other words, we assume participation in the program by nonparents will exactly make up for nonparticipation by parents.

Student Transfers to Nonpublic Schools: While the program will encourage some parents, particularly those with low incomes, to transfer their children to nonpublic schools, we believe the program is unlikely to cause a large movement of children from public to nonpublic schools.   For most parents, the rebate will total just $348, less than a tenth what the public schools spend per pupil.   Keeping their children in (improving) public schools is a way for parents to leverage their tax "contribution" to education by a factor of four-to-one.   Nonpublic schools will continue to have difficulty competing against such heavily subsidized schools.   Only those public schools that are truly failing to satisfy parents will be threatened by this program.   In scenarios 3a and 3b below, we project one child in twenty, and then one child in ten, transferring from public schools to nonpublic schools.   We believe either estimate overstates the likely rate of transfers, so these are pessimistic (or high cost) scenarios.

Contributions to Public Schools: Presently, three students out of four in Chicago attend public schools.   Since a mass exodus from the public schools following enactment of the program is unlikely, the parents of these children who choose to participate in the Education Rebate program will be making contributions to their local public school, not to nonpublic schools.   Nevertheless, in the scenarios below we will continue to assume that *every* contribution made under the program will be lost to the public school system.   The reader should note that this is an extreme scenario.

The Scenarios: With these assumptions, the following revenue diversions would occur:

1. If the parents of every child now enrolled in a nonpublic school in Chicago applies for, and receives, the maximum rebate:

    $348 x 126,000 = $44 million
    $$= 2.4 \text{ percent of budget.}$$

2. If every qualifying business applies for and receives a rebate equal to 10 percent of the business' education property tax liability (the maximum allowed by the plan):

    $250 million x .10 = $25 million
    $$= 1.4 \text{ percent of budget.}$$

3a. If 5 percent of students currently enrolled in the public schools are withdrawn and enrolled in qualifying nonpublic schools in Chicago, and their parents receive the maximum rebate:

    $348 x 21,000 = $7.3 million
    $$= .04 \text{ percent of budget.}$$

3b. If 10 percent of public school students were transferred to nonpublic schools, and their families receive the maximum rebate:

    $348 x 42,000 = $14.6 million
    $$= .08 \text{ percent of budget.}$$

The total diversion of funds if 5 percent of all public school children are enrolled in nonpublic schools (1 + 2 + 3a) would be $76.3 million, or 4.2 percent of the budget. The total diversion of funds if 10 percent of all public school children are enrolled in nonpublic schools (1 + 2 + 3b) would be $83.6 million, or 4.6 percent of the budget.

These estimates should remove any fear that Education Rebates would harm the public schools. The amount of funds redirected by individual parents and community members into nonpublic schools, even with these seemingly unrealistic assumptions, total less than 5 percent of the public school system's total annual budget.

Lost State Tax Revenues to the Public School System

Although Education Rebates would be unlikely to have a major effect on the Chicago Public Schools' *property* tax revenues, they may have an indirect effect on the system's *state* tax support. Public schools receive General State Aid based on their Total Weighted Average Daily Attendance. In 1988, this aid amounted to $2,057 per student, fully half the per-pupil spending by the schools. If the Education Rebate plan leads to a reduction in public school enrollment, it could lead to less state aid.

How large a threat to the public schools does this pose? The threat is minimized by the fact that children currently enrolled in nonpublic schools are already absent from the system's Average Daily Attendance. Only new transfers to nonpublic schools will affect the level of state aid. If no changes are made to the state aid formula, the Education Rebate plan would cost the Chicago Public Schools $43 million (2.4 percent of total budget) if one child in twenty leaves the system, or $86 million (4.8 percent of total budget) if one child in ten leaves.

In this scenario, the Chicago Public Schools' loss is the state's gain. The state would retain between $43 million and $86 million in previously allocated funds. This money could be used to facilitate implementation of the plan in Chicago by easing the financial hardship on schools that face swift changes in enrollment. Rather than reduce a school's general aid by $2,057 when a student transfers out, the state could continue to send the aid for one or two years, thereby enabling the school to project its next year's budget with some accuracy. This is a "win-win" situation, since the Chicago Public Schools get a short-term "windfall" of funds for students who are no longer enrolled, and the state is assured that its spending obligation is still tied to enrollment, not to budget levels of past years.

Cost Reduction Opportunities

The Board of Education experiences cost reduction opportunities when the number of children enrolled in its schools declines. The amount the public schools could save is roughly equal to the number of students who would transfer to nonpublic schools multiplied by $4,000, the amount currently spent on each student each year. (See note following Chapter Eleven concerning average and marginal cost.) Since the average *property tax revenue* loss for each child who leaves the public schools will probably be less than $400, the public schools are left with *more* money per student to spend.

Assume for now that the state aid formula is changed so that the total amount of state aid coming to the Chicago Public Schools is not affected by the plan. If 5 percent of public school students transfer to nonpublic schools, the public schools could lose $7.3 million in property tax revenues, but the public school cost of educating those children would have been $84 million (21,000 times $4,000), or over ten times that much. So the public schools would actually *benefit* from the program by having approximately $77 million more to spend on the students who are still enrolled in its schools. If fully 10 percent of the students now enrolled in the Chicago Public Schools transferred to schools elsewhere, the local revenue loss would be $14.6 million, the cost deferred would be $168 million, and the net benefit to the public schools would total $153 million.

If the state aid formula is not changed, the *combined* state and local revenue loss for the Chicago Public School system would be $50 million if 5 percent of the students transferred to other schools, and $100 million if 10 percent transferred. Even in these extreme scenarios, the cost savings opportunities caused by lower enrollment exceed the revenue loss. In the first case, the net benefit to the public schools would total $34 million; in the second case, $68 million.

These numbers suggest that the Education Rebate plan does not pose a threat to the viability of the public school system, and in fact provides a way to raise spending per pupil in the public schools without raising taxes. This higher spending could be as high as $364 per pupil, and could be applied to higher teachers' salaries, better instructional materials, or other areas. This will only occur, however, if the vast bureaucracy and administrative overhead of the system is scaled back as the number of pupils declines.

Systemwide Improvements and Efficiencies

In addition to the Education Rebate program's impact on the Chicago Public Schools' tax revenues and enrollment, another effect would be felt on the system's management and performance. The principal task of the Education Rebate program, as we have stressed in this book, is to create a new accountability and responsiveness to the public schools. By allowing parents to express their dissatisfaction by enrolling their children in nonpublic schools, the public schools will finally have an objective bottom line against which to measure their performance. With this information, public school administrators can embark on policies that will cut waste, restore educational quality, and win back the support of business and parents.

By allowing persons and companies to collect rebates for contributions made to *public* as well as nonpublic schools, the Education Rebate plan places public schools in competition with one another for a small fraction of the funds currently being distributed by the Central Administration. We would expect this competition to be lively, with schools using newsletters and even newspaper advertising to solicit contributions from parents and community members. Schools would strive to become more competitive by improving test results, offering courses for which parents express support, and welcoming community participation in school governance. Every member of a school's staff will realize that the school must win the confidence of parents and community members in order to secure extra funding for new projects or program improvements.

As was shown above, less than 5 percent of the central administration's total budget might be returned to the parents of children enrolled in nonpublic schools. Some additional amount would be returned to persons who made contributions to individual public schools, creating a competitive atmosphere within the public school system, but not depriving the public school system of funds.

About the Sponsors

United Republican Fund of Illinois and URF Education Foundation

The United Republican Fund of Illinois is a 54-year-old statewide political finance and advocacy organization based in Chicago. The Fund works to elect political candidates and establish public policies that promote free enterprise, strong families, limited government, and a vigilant national defense. The Board of Governors of the Fund believes that a Republican Party built on principle, and caring about people, will be a strong Republican Party. Membership in the Fund is open to all citizens regardless of race, creed, ethnicity, gender, or handicap. Its president is Kenneth T. Wright.

The URF Education Foundation is the nonpartisan affiliate of the United Republican Fund of Illinois, dedicated to research and education on public policy matters of interest to people of varying political persuasions. *We Can Rescue Our Children* is the outgrowth of the Foundation's Education Policy Initiative, begun in February 1987. Other Foundation projects include distribution of the video production, "Which Way America?" which captures highlights of a recent Chicago debate between William F. Buckley Jr. and former Senator George McGovern; policy discussion groups; and a new conservative reference library open to the general public.

The Heartland Institute

Founded in 1984 in Chicago, The Heartland Institute exists to encourage the discussion of state and local public policies that promote economic growth and improve the quality of public services. More than forty prominent academics and research professionals participate in research and review procedures for The Heartland Institute, making it one of the most respected research organizations of its kind in the nation. Heartland research has been quoted or reprinted thousands of times in newspapers and journals across the country, and Heartland researchers frequently appear as guests on radio and television programs. Research from The Heartland Institute is brought to audiences in Wisconsin through Heartland's Milwaukee-based affiliate, Heartland Wisconsin. A Detroit-area office is expected to open in early 1989. The Heartland Institute and its affiliates are strictly nonpartisan and accept no funding from government agencies. Contributions are tax deductible under Section 501(c)3 of the Internal Revenue Code. Its president is David H. Padden.

The Illinois Council on Democratic Policy

The Illinois Council on Democratic Policy is a statewide Democratic policy research and review group. Formed recently, the Illinois Council works with the Democratic Party and with Democratic members of the Illinois legislature to develop policy initiatives and critique legislation. It makes its findings known through the Democratic Party, Democratic candidates, and the press. The Council's recent activities include creation of study groups on such important Illinois issues as education, economic development, the environment, the criminal justice system, transportation, and mental health. Its resources are available to all Democratic candidates and officials. The chairman of the council is Michael J. Bakalis.

HOW YOU CAN RESCUE YOUR CHILDREN
and Cure Chicago's Public School Crisis

To change the system we must change people's minds. That is why it is so important to get this book quickly into the hands of your neighbors, your community leaders, and your legislators. Through the generosity of donors to the United Republican Fund of Illinois and URF Education Foundation, copies of *WE CAN RESCUE OUR CHILDREN: The Cure for Chicago's Public School Crisis* are available at quantity discounts. These cosponsors also have agreed to pay Illinois sales tax on your order.

PRICES

1 copy	$ 1.75	50 copies	$ 35.00
3 copies	$ 5.00	100 copies	$ 60.00
5 copies	$ 7.50	500 copies	$275.00
10 copies	$12.50	1000 copies	$500.00
25 copies	$25.00		

GREEN HILL PUBLISHERS, INC.
P. O. Box 738
Ottawa, Illinois 61350

Please send me postpaid _____ copies of *WE CAN RESCUE OUR CHILDREN: The Cure for Chicago's Public School Crisis*. Enclosed is a check or money order for $_____.

Please charge my VISA___ MASTERCARD___
Number _____
Expiration Date _____

Signature _____
Name _____
Street or Box _____
City _____
State _____ Zip _____